The Last Mass of Padre Pio

The Last Mass of Padre Pio

The Secret Soul of the Stigmatic Saint

Based on newly found documents
never before published

Alessandro Gnocchi
Mario Palmaro

Translated from the Italian by Marianna Gattozzi

Angelus
Press

PO Box 217 | St. Marys, KS 66536

Original edition: *L' ultima messa di padre Pio. L'anima segreta del santo delle stigmate* © 2010 - EDIZIONI PIEMME Spa
20145 Milano - Via Tiziano, 32, Italy
info@edizpiemme.it - www.edizpiemme.it

Library of Congress Cataloging-in-Publication Data

Names: Gnocchi, Alessandro, author. | Palmaro, Mario, 1968- author.
Title: The last mass of Padre Pio : the secret soul of the stigmatic saint /
Alessandro Gnocchi, Mario Palmaro ; translated from the Italian by
Marianna Gattozzi.
Other titles: Ultima messa di Padre Pio. English
Description: 1st [edition]. | Kansas City : Angelus Press, 2019. | "Based on
newly found documents never before published." | Includes bibliographical
references.
Identifiers: LCCN 2019012539 | ISBN 9781937843694 (pbk.)
Subjects: LCSH: Pio, of Pietrelcina, Saint, 1887-1968. |
Capuchins--Italy--Biography. | Stigmatics--Italy--Biography.
Classification: LCC BX4705.P49 G6613 2019 | DDC 282.092 [B] --dc23
LC record available at https://lccn.loc.gov/2019012539

ANGELUS PRESS
PO Box 217
ST. MARYS, KANSAS 66536
PHONE (816) 753-3150
FAX (816) 753-3557
ORDER LINE 1-800-966-7337
www.angeluspress.org

ISBN 978-1-937843-69-4
FIRST PRINTING—November 2019
SECOND PRINTING—August 2020

Printed in the United States of America

Contents

Chapter 2

Chapter 3

Chapter 4

Chapter 5

Notes from the translator

All biblical quotations have been taken from the Douay-Rheims version, (TAN Books & Publishers, Inc., Rockford, IL, 1989).

Latin words and phrases have been translated, except those in common use among Catholics.

This book often refers to persons and events perhaps unfamiliar to those outside of Italy and to a greater extent outside of Europe. In such cases, some minimal information, not included in the original text, has been provided which may be helpful in placing people and places in their proper contexts.

Foreword

It has been nearly 50 years since the passing of Padre Pio, the only priest known to have ever received the full stigmata. After suffering many years of trials and indignities by those who did not understand the miraculous nature of his apostolate here on earth, this holy monk was forced to witness the advent of the Conciliar reforms which plunged the Catholic Church into the profound crisis from which She has yet to extricate herself. Today, following his canonization by Pope John Paul II in 2002, Padre Pio is often held up as a beacon of humility with very little being said outside of traditional Catholic circles concerning his devotion to the traditional Latin Mass and his resistance to *aggiornamento*—the "updating" of the Church, including her religious orders, in the wake of Vatican II.

While hundreds of works on Padre Pio are now available in numerous languages, Alessandro Gnocchi and Mario Palmaro's *The Last Mass of Padre Pio* deepens our understanding of this mystic, particularly his devotion to the Mass. Even before the close of Vatican II and the promulgation of the *Novus Ordo Missae*, liturgical reformers within the Church had already begun to propose alterations to the Mass, including celebrating portions of it in the vernacular. Already sensing the great danger these reforms would bring, Padre Pio appealed directly to Pope Paul VI to be dispensed from celebrating a degraded form of the Roman Rite.

It was surely a blessing that God called Padre Pio home to his Heavenly reward before the full demolition of the Roman Church's liturgy could take place. Had Padre Pio lived to see the full incorporation of the New Mass into the life of the Church and the heinous abuses attached to it, there can be little doubt that he would have resisted celebrating it. Although Padre Pio's life was marked by profound obedience even in the face of injustices, he knew—as Archbishop Marcel Lefebvre knew—the centrality of the Holy Sacrifice to the life of both the priest and the Mystical Body as a whole.

As this book details, Padre Pio's entire religious life was spent conforming himself to Christ, to truly being an *Alter Christus*. His gifts of chastity, humility, patience, and love were also marked by a willingness to suffer spiritually for the good of the entire Church. It was in the Mass that Padre Pio found the strength to carry out his work for Christ. It was in the Mass that the holy Friar found a pathway to contemplating the great mystery of Our Lord's Passion and the salvific work of the Cross.

Before proceeding to the main text of *The Last Mass of Padre Pio*, a few additional words are in order. While the book is imbued with a great love for Padre Pio and the traditional Latin Mass, it is a work which was written and published originally outside of the auspices of the Society of Saint Pius X. As such, readers should take care not to conflate certain opinions of the authors with the official positions of the Society itself. However, because this book enters into the traditional liturgical life of Padre Pio with unprecedented detail and sympathy, Angelus Press has seen fit to publish it without cumbersome edits and rewrites.

Fr. Dominique Bourmaud, SSPX

In the Devil's Territory

Heaven assigns to Padre Pio a mysterious mission whereby
he will have to oppose the snares of the antichrist and
suffer for love of the Church

San Giovanni Rotondo, Thursday March 19, 2009
Feast of St. Joseph, 11:30 am

"Not a good starting point." This first entry we jotted down in
our notebook is dejected, but precise—our journey into the interior
world of Padre Pio, undertaken to investigate his total dedication to
the Mass, and how and why he traveled his painful path of Christ's
sufferings, begins with our stumbling into an enigma.

We had begun at San Giovanni Rotondo, in southeastern Italy,
where the stigmatic friar lived during the longest period of his
life and where his mortal remains are kept. But soon we began to
sense that the answers to our quest might be found elsewhere when
we overheard the conversation of a group of pilgrims leaving the
new church dedicated to our saint, the liturgical monster built by
Renzo Piano. Some of them said, with no hesitation whatsoever,
that this glorification of cement and modernity is worth less than
one square inch of the painting they had seen the previous day in
Campobasso. There, for sure, one had the unequivocal feeling of
being in front of the saint and his secret. These were their exact
words: "the saint and his secret."

"Not a good starting point." This idea had come to us quickly,
so much so that it became a specific entry in our notebook. The
pilgrims, however, disappeared in a flash, and we were unable to
ask them for even a bit of explanation. We had no idea of the pre-

cise subject and details of the painting or fresco they were talking about. Any mention of it in the vast literature on the Padre must be subtle. Possibly they were talking about a painting located in the shrine of Santa Maria del Monte in Campobasso, where Padre Pio had arrived in 1905, at the age of 18, before taking his solemn vows. Perhaps, just because of this, we should start from there.

If we had begun our journey with the cautious footsteps of scholars, we quickly realized we must expand our strategy by including, at certain intervals, the silent movement of detectives and the slow rhythmic tread of pilgrims. One can walk over a ground of mystery only after a previous terrain of discovery has been examined, by patiently approaching one territory of evidence after another, in careful succession, until a certain path, which men cannot navigate on their own, becomes evident. Along this ground of mystery one is not allowed to wander, but must continue, adding to that which appeared previously, moving successively forward. Then, how many expanses must we encounter until we can stand upon, even for one instant, in the story of Padre Pio, the truth of the Padre's mission of struggle and suffering which lies beneath the surface of this modernized saint?

A picture the artist did not want to paint

Campobasso, Thursday March 19, 2009, 2:30 pm

From San Giovanni Rotondo westward to Campobasso the road stretches for 80 miles over difficult terrain and lasts for two good hours. Throughout the journey we feared we would find ourselves to have been so naïve for believing the gossip of a bunch of strangers. But then, in the Sanctuary of Santa Maria del Monte, we indeed did find the painting. It is a rare example of valuable contemporary art and represents the apparition of the Virgin Mary to a young Fra Pio; the Virgin is pointing out to the youth the figure of Jesus ascending Calvary while carrying His cross.

The work is located on the wall beyond the altar of a little side chapel dedicated to the saint, which is carved on the right hand side of the entrance of the sanctuary. The words of the pilgrims in San Giovani Rotondo were absolutely accurate: The clarity of the scene depicted reveals an event that had really happened, and, in its sobriety and austerity, frames and highlights a dialogue perceived only by the two main figures in the picture. "The saint and his secret": these were the words pronounced by our involuntary informers. This might well also be the title of the painting.

As we later learned, Padre Pellegrino from Sant'Elia a Pianisi, the friar who remained close to Padre Pio until the last moments of his earthy life, was the one who had continuously asked, with an almost annoying persistence, that the artist Amedeo Trivisonno paint the event. In the year 1971, Padre Pellegrino explained to the artist:

> Amedeo, here the Blessed Mother appeared to Padre Pio several times. You, who are such a religious man, must paint a picture representing the most important of all these apparitions, the one that took place on the day of the Assumption in 1905. This was the apparition prompting the Padre to become an *Alter Christus*.

Trivisonno, an artist well known in Italy and in surrounding regions, was, most importantly in this case, a very religious man. He was fond of the Capuchins and he loved Padre Pio, but deep down he was reticent to undertake this particular work. The nature of the revelation from Padre Pellegrino left him unsettled, but the friar was so persistent that in September Trivisonno started the work in his studio in Florence, and by May of the following year, he finished the *Apparition of the Madonna to Padre Pio*.

The level of detail exhibited in the painting indicates that Padre Pellegrino, in disclosing the event to his artist friend, revealed all he had gathered through his close relationship with Padre Pio. This evidently explains why Trivisonno was unsettled by the fact that a young man called to be priest had been asked to become *Alter Christus*. Although the call to the priesthood is explicitly that of becoming conformed to Christ, it was apparent that Fra Pio had been asked much more than that: after the vision of 1903, which had indicated he would undergo a lifelong and continuous battle with the devil, he then was asked, in the apparition of 1905, depicted in the painting, to share the Cross and to be united to the divine sacrifice to the point of suffering in his body the very pains of the Redeemer.

That the Saint of Pietrelcina is the first priest in the history of the Church to receive the stigmata, the seal of total dedication to the passion of Christ by reliving the crucifixion at Calvary, testifies to the uniqueness and greatness of what had been asked of Padre Pio. All of this, in the language of the Catholic Church, can be expressed by one single concept: "The Holy Mass."

The Mass cannot change

Truly, it was not an injudicious choice, that of placing our trust in the conversation of the pilgrims at San Giovanni Rotondo. Their subject, that young friar contemplating the Madonna, with his open arms waiting to be nailed onto the Cross which Christ is carrying to Calvary, really conveys the sensation of witnessing a profound event from which one can fully comprehend the attachment of Padre Pio to the Mass. The scene explains his burning desire to stay as long as possible at the altar, the celebrations lasting hours and hours in the pangs of the crucifixion and in the contemplation of the consecrated host, and his urgency to offer as many Masses as possible in reparation for the neglect and indifference with which so many—too many—priests celebrated them. And, with even greater clarity, one can understand the attachment of the saint to the immutability of the rite with which Jesus, each time a priest consecrates the bread and wine, makes Himself present as the perfect victim on the altar.

Later, as an aged Capuchin friar, the mere thought of the premonitory symptoms of the liturgical reform which would take effect in 1969, after his death, was sufficient to raise in him a holy horror. Throughout his life the holy friar had been obedient even unto martyrdom, but at this time the only request he dared to put forth to the authorities of the Church was to be exempted from the novelties of the impending liturgical reform. And he directed his plea to the very pope who would issue the new missal: Pope Paul VI. His was not the whim of an old eccentric who was confined to the past and who sentimentalized it in the present; it was the cry of a man of God who could see the destruction on the horizon of the future.

"My mission," he had confided to Luigi Peroni, director of his prayer groups, "will end when on earth the Mass will no longer be celebrated." And on other occasions he said: "The world could even exist without sunlight, but not without the Holy Mass." What did Heaven show to that young friar on the feast of the Assumption in 1905, and later in the many subsequent celestial visions, which produced the Padre's messages which were so emphatic and disturbing?

Although a precise answer is impossible, what we can gather is an inkling of the incommensurability of the Holy Sacrifice of the Mass to any of the greatest things we poor creatures can imagine, an incommensurability sufficient to justify the humiliations, the sufferings, the abuses that Padre Pio accepted from so many churchmen throughout his life in the Church: He was treated as an impostor and as one hysterically unbalanced because of his stigmata, as a thief and profiteer because of his deeds of charity towards those who suffer, as a plagiarist and necromancer because of the long hours spent in the confessional, and as a bigot and fundamentalist because of his love and devotion for the holy Catholic doctrine—all of this for the greater glory of the Church, immaculate Mystical Body of Our Lord Jesus Christ, who gave him daily the privilege to be faithful to his mission of ascending the altar and dying once more on the Cross with Jesus.

We know, however, that until the end of time, the Church will always have within its walls someone who attempts to obscure the light of truth, someone who, as the ultimate sign of aggression to the immaculate Bride of Christ, will endeavor to destroy the Mass and obstruct the sacrifice that holds together the world. Padre Pio very soon had become aware of such dangers.

The master stroke of the Enemy

Padre Pio had received with sorrow the painful confidences of Christ, who referred to the priests as "butchers" who unworthily celebrated His death on the Cross. But, as the years went by, he saw that the danger would become ever more looming, more real, and more widespread. His isolated personal indignities, as numerous as they were, no longer satisfied the Enemy's desire and strategy. The saint's spiritual antennae caught a plan which would change the very nature of the Mass. This plan, if successful, would divert even good priests from the essence of their holy ministry by deceiving them into thinking they were continuing to serve the Lord: zealous ministers of God who were driven into error because of their "obedience," resulting in the propagation of the infection all the way to the faithful. Truly a master stroke! Whereas Modernism at the beginning of the century was unsuccessful, remaining within its books and treatises as an elitist phenomenon, Neo-modernism would instead succeed, becoming a popular trend thanks to a new liturgy. In the Anti-Christ's plan, the crisis of the Mass would impart an epoch-making turn in the crisis of the Church, already weakened by openly heretical theologies. At that time, a man above suspicion, Jacques Maritain, in his 1966 book *Le Paysan de la Garonne* (*The Peasant of the Garonne*), would say that, compared to the theologies producing the new liturgy, Modernism had been just a hay fever.

These were not the fears of a poor visionary, but the keen and lucid perception of the dangers that the Church would have to face until the end of time. In addition, since the mid-1960s, these perceptions increasingly became realities. In the 19th century, Dom Prosper Gueranger, restorer of the Benedictine Order and scholar of the Liturgy, described the crisis in a series of conferences on the Holy Mass which he presented to his monks:

> From the terminology used by the Church we understand how much the Holy Mass surpasses personal devotions. Therefore, the Mass must be kept first among all of them, and

its intentions must be respected. This is how the Church makes all its members partakers of this great sacrifice; therefore, should the Sacred Sacrifice of the Mass cease, it will not be long before we will fall back into the abyss of depravity where the pagans once were, and this would be the work of the Antichrist. He will use all means he can to impede the celebration of the Holy Mass, so that this great counterbalance might be abolished, and thus God will put an end to all things, having no more reason to keep them in existence.

During the last years of his life, Padre Pio was weighed down by the realization that the words of Dom Gueranger were becoming more and more manifest in the world. The clearer his realization became, though, the more he found himself surrounded by people ready to obscure it. People spoke, sometimes even agreeably, about the uniqueness of his Mass, for which, however, they saw no reason, as if it were a variation on a theme which was allowed to become ever freer in form and interpretation, rather than an established canon necessary to follow. Even less the people spoke about Padre Pio's attachment to the Mass that was "the rite of all time," the Mass as a liturgy with roots spanning two millennia; instead they spoke as if, for him, his role of "hanging on the Cross like Christ" could be reduced to that of "presiding at an assembly." As Padre Pio aged, he lost more and more of his strength, and his greater realization of this discrepancy regarding the Mass forced him, a saint devoted to suffering, into a level of suffering even more difficult because he could contemplate in the change the devastating danger for a countless number of souls.

The Calvary of Padre Pio
and the rediscovered archive

Rome, April 30, 2005, Feast of St. Pius V[1]

At this point, we must go back four years, to 2005, because our journey really began on an afternoon in Rome, eleven days after the election of Pope Benedict XVI. Not far from St. Peter's Square, a bookstall featuring used books prominently displayed two large volumes bound with red cloth and decorated in gold: *The Calvary of Padre Pio*. The author, Giuseppe Pagnossin, was a businessman from Padua and a spiritual son of the Saint of Pietrelcina. Mr. Pagnossin had devolved all his possessions and most of his life to defending the Padre from the calumnies and persecutions raised against him. A quick look at the two volumes immediately revealed that they were a veritable gold mine of unknown documents, photocopies, pictures, and a biography of the saint written in a manner more accurately detailed than no other had been. No indication of a publisher or a printer appeared. I had to buy it!

Some time passed. On my desk among the files of the books I was currently writing, no file named "Project Padre Pio" had yet existed, but those two large volumes stored in the shelves did require some attention. Then, an important thought came to mind: if Pagnossin decided that so much material was worth printing, he must have had much more, a real archive—but where is it? This question became more and more intriguing after I discovered that *The Calvary of Padre Pio* had remained unpublished, with only a few copies having been distributed by the writer himself. This discovery generated a new question: If Pagnossin does have an archive, what else might it contain?

A bit of luck, some friends, and some experience led me to learn that the family of the Paduan businessman had donated the

---

[1] The authors are following the reformed calendar of the *Novus Ordo*. The feast of St. Catherine of Siena is celebrated on April 30th in the traditional calendar of the Catholic Church, whereas the feast day of St. Pius V is May 5.

archive to the Society of Saint Pius X and that it was stored in Albano Laziale, the residence of the District Superior of the Society in Italy. The archive was there simply because Giuseppe Pagnossin, after Padre Pio's death, looked for someone linked, as the Saint of Pietrelcina had been, to the Mass and to the Catholic Doctrine of all time; Pagnossin found it in the person of Archbishop Marcel Lefebvre, founder of the Society of Saint Pius X. Pagnossin was not intimidated by the accusations poured out upon the French archbishop because of his opposition to the innovations within the Church beginning in the 60s. Nor was he frightened by the canonical consequences of this matter, which culminated in the excommunication *latae sententiae* in 1988, revoked only later in 2009.[2] Rather, like many other spiritual sons of Padre Pio, he found a safe harbor in Tradition, where, as a token of the fidelity to the doctrine and the Mass of all time, a profound devotion to St. Pius X was alive, the pope in whose honor the young Francesco Forgione[3] of Pietrelcina took his religious name.

Among the notations in his dossier, Pagnossin clarifies his position:

> But the attack of Satan, even more painfully, also takes place within the Church, where the very successors of the Apostles contest tradition, dogma, and pope, based on the supremely false reasoning of the daredevil Lutheran argument of free interpretation understood as the negation of the revealed word, in a dialectic that has nothing left of orthodox doctrinal inspiration, but that has all of extemporaneous subversive inventiveness. Thus is repeated within the bosom of the Church of Christ the heretical phenomenon of the protest against the tradition of truth, which had happened in the Sanhedrin regarding the truth of scriptural prophecies.

---

[2] This is not quite exact: the excommunication was for consecrating bishops, not for opposition to Church innovation.

[3] Francesco Forgione was the secular name of Padre Pio.

The Friar and the Archbishop

Albano Laziale, Thursday October 1, 2009, Feast of Saint Theresa
of The Child Jesus[4]

Some time was needed, and long-standing commitments had to be fulfilled before a file entitled "Project Padre Pio" appeared on my desk and the archive of Giuseppe Pagnossin appeared on a wide wall, which became covered by the archive's books, binders full of documents, memoirs and re-enactments, photos, and films. We needed to start digging into it. At first, we were curious about the story of the source of this collection and the place where it came to reside, and about the meeting of Monsignor[5] Lefebvre and Padre Pio, a meeting often spoken of, but never reported in the biographies of the saint. Such a meeting is noted only by Cristina Siccardi in her recent well-documented book *Mons. Marcel Lefebvre. Nel nome della Verita* [*Archbishop Marcel Lefebvre: In the Name of Truth*]. Their meeting continues to be removed from the pages of chronicles and history for fear of having the Saint of Pietrelcina labeled as a "traditionalist." We need to realize that a meeting between him and Monsignor Lefebvre was completely natural and coherent, given the attachment of both men to the Mass and the Catholic doctrine of all time, and given the resulting misunderstandings and the persecutions received by each from within the Church.

In an archive folder laconically labeled "Mons. Lefebvre" was an account with photos of their meeting, and among these, a clip of the official bulletin of the Casa Sollievo della Sofferenza [House for the Relief of Suffering], the hospital founded by the saint in San Giovanni Rotondo. The note is dated March 31, 1967, the Thursday after Easter:

---

[4] The authors are following the reformed calendar of the *Novus Ordo*. The feast of St. Theresa of the Child Jesus is celebrated on October 3 in the traditional calendar of the Catholic Church, whereas October 1 is the feast of St. Remigius.

[5] In Italian the common use of the more generic title of "Monsignor" is often used instead of the more specific one, in this case "Archbishop."

Padre Pio received the visit of Monsignor Marcel Lefebvre, Archbishop of Synnada (Phrygia), General Superior of the Congregation of The Holy Ghost Fathers, and also counselor of the Congregation for the Propagation of the Faith. Monsignor Lefebvre, after attending the Mass celebrated by Padre Pio, had a meeting with him (see picture). The Congregation of the Holy Ghost Fathers is 264 years old. The General house has recently been transferred from Paris to Rome.

In addition to the photo published in the bulletin, which testifies to the cordiality of the meeting in which the Archbishop asked the Capuchin saint for his benediction for the imminent general chapter of the Congregation of the Holy Ghost Fathers, another photo shows Padre Pio devoutly kissing the ring of the successor of the apostles. In one of his memoirs Monsignor Lefebvre recalls:

> I asked Padre Pio for a blessing, which he refused to give while asking to humbly kiss my pastoral ring, and insisting, on the contrary, to receive himself a blessing from me.

Worlds very far away

The remainder of the archives were like an immense sea on which floated little unpublished pearls: the saint's dedications on books and missals, brief prayers, reflections. There was also the photocopy of the unabridged version of his brief mystical treatise now published in a revised format as an appendix to the fourth volume of his *Epistolary*.

Of course, there were more than these items, but what I looked for, literally groped for, pertained to Padre Pio and the Holy Mass. The well-trained eye quickly identified materials published elsewhere. Pagnossin had certainly conserved, photographed, and transcribed all that he could find. There was enough material there truly to enlighten us on the subject, so much material, in fact, that one had to ask why no one until now ever thought of publishing it.

Among the never-published material, there were savory and consoling confirmations of all that Padre Pio said and did regarding the Holy Sacrifice. For example, in the dedication on the front page of the Missal belonging to Angelina Buratti, of Venice, dated 1958:

> While participating in the Holy Mass, renew your faith and meditate on the victim who immolates Himself for you to the divine justice, to placate it and propitiate it. Never leave the altar before pouring out tears of sorrow and love to Jesus Crucified for your eternal salvation. The Sorrowful Mother will keep you company and will sweetly inspire you.
>
> *P. Pio Capuchin*

In a note to one of his spiritual sons he repeated:

> While attending the Holy Mass you must be totally focused on the tremendous mystery that unfolds under your own eyes: the Redemption of your friendship and the reconciliation with God.
>
> *P. Pio Capuchin*

These words are a true treatise on the Holy Mass summarized in a few lines which would help today's modern seminarians. Likewise, it would be of much more consolation to be able to read on the holy cards for the new ordinands something resembling the prayer suggested by Padre Pio, written on a note preserved by Pagnossin, on the occasion of the consecration of his sister Suor Pia:

> *Tenui eum nec dimittam.* [6]
> Oh Lord, Who in your goodness
> has raised me to the sublime
> honor of being your bride:
> Grant me perpetual fidelity,
> pour in abundance your graces
> upon my Sisters, upon my beloved parents,
> and upon all who participate
> in my joy.

---

[6] "I held him and will not let him go" (Cant. 3:4).

To us accustomed to the modern Church, these words seem like a message reaching us from worlds very far away, yet they are the fruits of the simple and immutable faith professed for all time by the Church of Christ. But nowadays this message seems difficult to understand, because the doctrinal uncertainty of today, which often ends up in true heresy, demonstrates the absolute need and purpose for the atoning mission of Padre Pio. If many of the Padre's spiritual sons, because of their fidelity to the Mass of all time, had been rejected by the majority of the churchmen of the 1960s who had taken the new path, it is easy to suppose that the first stigmatic priest in history would have foreseen the crisis and would suffer as a consequence. It was a dramatic event never seen before because, for the first time, the Mystical Body of Christ was lacerated through the attempt to revolutionize the sacrifice offered on the altar.

The numerous little pearls hidden in the archive of Pagnossin reveal that Padre Pio, himself a man of sacrifice, had molded his spiritual children into standard-bearers of the Mass. Many speeches from him to them were unnecessary: his example and the brief reminders he sent to them on short notes, dedications on books, or warnings written on missals were sufficient. In this way, he prepared them to face difficult times known only to the divine wisdom; he made them careful sowers who would not scatter the good seeds he would use until the end: "My mission will end when on the earth the Holy Mass will no longer be celebrated."

Fighting against the Enemy

Springes (Bolzano), Sunday January 31, 2010, Feast of Saint John Bosco

Father Josef von Zieglauer, the retired pastor of this small village 15 minutes away from Bressanone, had just finished celebrating the 6:30 am Mass in the indescribable Chapel of the Holy Sepulcher when someone passing by the chapel asked about the future of the Holy Sacrifice. One of the faithful, in a common German which contrasted dramatically with the liturgical Latin, gave the immediate reply: "The Antichrist wants to destroy the Mass. When the Antichrist will be here, the Mass will be no longer. Read the writings of St. Irenaeus."

The words of St. Irenaeus of Lyon, in his treatise *Against the Heresies,* are hard to forget, even by those in more remote areas, focused on the timelessness of the Mass. The importance of the words lies in their connection with the work of Padre Pio. Such a link reveals itself in all its disquieting evidence. "For this reason," explains St. Irenaeus, talking about the coming of the Antichrist,

> Daniel says: "The sanctuary will be desolate: sin has been offered instead of sacrifice, and justice has been thrown to the ground. He did it and he was successful."

St. Irenaeus also writes:

> The angel Gabriel [...] then, in order to indicate the length of the tyranny, during which the saints who offer to God a pure sacrifice will be put to flight, declares: "And in the middle of the week the sacrifice and the libation will be suppressed and in the temple the abomination of desolation will take place, and until the end of time the desolation will be accomplished." [...] the things [...] that Daniel prophesied regarding the end of times have been proved by The Lord, when He says: "When you will see the abomination of desolation prophesied by Daniel."

The abomination of desolation prophesied by Daniel, confirmed by Our Lord, and recalled by St. Irenaeus, is, undoubtedly, a world without the Mass. We don't know what heavenly signs were given to Padre Pio which indicated to him how and when such event will take place. Certainly, the strength and urgency with which he upheld the Mass of all time in the last years of his life cannot be underestimated.

In this regard, a great and troubling suggestion comes from Dom Gueranger writing in the 19th century in his conferences on the Holy Sacrifice: "In the *Communicantes,* as well as in the *Confiteor,* St. Joseph's name is not mentioned, because the devotion to this blessed saint had been reserved for the last times." It is interesting to notice that the name of St. Joseph was added in the Canon under the pontificate of John XXIII by the decree *De S. Ioseph Nomine Canone Missae Inserendo*, November 13, 1962. Far from attempting to deduce the coming of the last times from this least cue, we must nevertheless ponder the mission given to Padre Pio from Heaven, especially in relation to his role as fighter of the enemy. Mother Eleonora Francesca Foresti, founder of the Franciscan Sisters of the Adoration, whose cause for beatification is underway, knew the stigmatic saint. In her *Diary* she reveals that by his prayers Italy was preserved from the Communist revolution of 1920. Then, she tells us what Jesus revealed to her about the uniqueness of such a man:

> The soul of Padre Pio is an impregnable fortress, is a wine cellar where I freely inebriate myself. It is a most clear sky where the angels mirror their face in wonder. It is a honeycomb! It is my refuge from men's ungratefulness. It is a looking glass of my soul where my image mirrors, like the most pure ray of the sun through the purest crystal! My voice in him is like the echo between two mountains!
>
> His speech is sweet and sharp! [...] it is mysterious like mine: it comforts you and crushes you. It has my very strength, because, I, Jesus, live in him. His spirit diffuses like a fluid. His gestures, his word, his look, are more effective than a deep discourse of a great orator. I enhance all that comes from him. He is the masterpiece of my mercy. I bestowed upon him all the gifts of my Spirit, more than to any other creature. He is the perfect imitator of me, my host, my altar, my sacrifice, my glory!

Non praevalebunt

Jesus reassured his followers regarding the destiny of the Catholic Church with His *non praevalebunt*,[7] by which it is nevertheless divine teaching that where there is Christ, until the end of

---

[7] "Shall not prevail" (subject is the gates of Hell) (Mt. 16:18).

time, there will always be on earth a presence of some antichrist: a presence of varying power and effectiveness, but always active. In the second letter to the Thessalonians, when St. Paul talks about the son of perdition, he does not use ambiguities to describe the adversary who rises above all that pertains to God. "You know now what holds him back," says the apostle in the ever splendid and Catholic version of Abbot Giuseppe Ricciotti,[8] "so that he will manifest himself only at the opportune time. The mystery of iniquity is already in action; only there is now he who holds him and will hold him until he will be eliminated."

The apparition of the Antichrist, then, meets the opposition of an obstacle and of someone who delays him, called in Greek Katéchon. According to St. Thomas Aquinas, the obstacle to the coming of the Antichrist mentioned by St. Paul consists of mankind's union with and submission to the Roman Church, seat and center of the Catholic Faith, evolved from the ancient earthly Roman Empire. But, because of God's magnanimity, next to this obstacle, there is a custodian, the Katéchon, whose mission it is to watch and guard it. Such a custodian is the pope, the vicar of Jesus Christ.

The priest Agostino Lémann in his essay *The Antichrist* explains:

> As long as the custodian will be acknowledged, respected, obeyed, the obstacle will hold, society will remain faithful to the spiritual Roman Empire and to the Catholic Faith. But if such custodian, the pope, will be ignored, set aside, rejected, the obstacle will disappear at the same time with him and the Antichrist will be free to manifest himself.

Legions of Catholic thinkers have attempted, with plausible reasoning, to discover the identity of the Katéchon, even though sometimes their conclusions differed. It would now be inopportune to yield to the temptation of inserting Padre Pio's name into

---

[8] Abbot Giuseppe Ricciotti, C. R. L. (1890-1964), was an Italian canon regular, Biblical scholar, and archeologist. He is mainly famous for his book *The Life of Christ* (*Wikipedia*).

the list of those hypotheses. But it is difficult not to read in the framework of the divine plan of opposition to the Enemy Padre Pio's life of prayer, sacrifice, and struggle, of which the convent of San Giovanni Rotondo became for a long time the hidden stage.

The last Mass of Padre Pio

San Giovanni Rotondo, March 19, 2010, Feast of St. Joseph.

We had to return here, then. And we returned with the same questions Giuseppe Pagnossin asked himself at the end of his reflections:

> Where shall we go, in the dark hour? Only toward the Faith of *non praevalebunt*! We must go toward the Faith of the word that "will not pass," not even when Heaven and earth will have passed; we must go toward the Faith of the shed blood, because, as Padre Pio recalls, "souls are not given as a gift; they must be bought, and do not ignore how much they cost Jesus. Now we have to pay for them still with the same currency."

Who nowadays has bought back with blood the souls from Satan, from protest, from "emancipation"? History says that among those who "paid the ransom" there is Padre Pio of Pietrelcina, the "great merchant."

Is he the "new St. Francis" expected by Pius XII? Is he the "needed one of this century" called to "the most high mission" of purchasing souls in a continuous agony that costs blood and suffering? ("I want to live by dying so that from death eternal life may come.") Is he the one who renews the syllogism of St. Paul: "I am crucified with Christ on the Cross; therefore it is not I who live, but Christ who lives in me?" Is he the one who re-proposes, at a time of greatest danger, the whole orthodoxy of revealed wisdom; the redeeming mystery of the Mass, of the Eucharist; the power of the rosary; the baptismal virtue of Confession; the redemptive value of suffering; the sanctity of the priesthood; the rigorous intransigence to sin; the "total imitation" of Christ for the glory of God, for the honor of the Capuchin Order?

Is he the one we had to wait for in the fear of the times, so that he could console us in the time of fear, by restoring "all the things that count to Your eyes": faith where there is disbelief, hope where there is despair, love where there is hatred, by invoking, like Moses, mercy between the infinite justice of God and the malice of men?

It was entirely necessary to return to San Giovanni Rotondo in order to verify the accuracy of our solution to this heavenly puzzle discovered the previous year, after we recorded in our notebook "Not a good starting point," and saw the painting of Padre Pio's 1905 vision. It was necessary that one more date be entered in our notebook: "Sunday, September 22, 1968, Feast of St. Maurice." Our journey began again from there, the day of the last Mass of Padre Pio.

PART ONE

TOWARD THE LORD

CHAPTER 1

Laying Down on the Altar for the Last Time

Padre Pio, for supreme obedience,
sacrifices his life and renders glory to God,
but is misunderstood by men

San Giovanni Rotondo, September 22, 1968.

It is only five o'clock in the morning and here, today, it looks as if there will be room only for a crowd, the crowd of a feast day: a chattering, curious, imploring, devout crowd. This is the peak hour for the international meeting of the prayer groups. It is the hour of the Mass celebrated by Padre Pio, the founder of these groups.

What did all these people come here to see? A reed shaken by the wind, a man clothed in soft garments, a prophet? Never mind. Today, whoever will look at the Padre with lively attention will have an almost physical perception of being on Calvary, at the place and the time of Jesus's tormented execution.

Some shout, some pray, some tremble, some fret. Here are the faithful, the disciples—and the executioners. And here is the victim, stretched on the Cross, meek and ready for the extreme sacrifice, the gift of his own life. Padre Pio surrendered to the will of men, in extreme obedience to God. His hands, tormented by the stigmata for 50 years, are miraculously turning snow-white and pure like a host, ready to be pierced by nails for the last time.

Entering into the church lit by the spotlights, a flood of people has barged in and filled the nave, the women's gallery, the choir loft, the confessionals, and now overflows outside, into the square of the convent. The tide moves in waves, swallowing up the police-men who are unable to contain it. All is ongoing, as journalists and photographers try to catch as much as they can of the event: shortly, surrounded by an enormous and electrified crowd, the stigmatic friar will celebrate a High Mass.

The Padre is about to die

In reality, the Padre is near death. He has little more than 20 hours of life left. Yesterday he could not find the strength to come down to the church, and he was able only to receive Communion in his cell. "It is over, it is over…" he told the confreres who attended him. The crowd does not yet know anything about this: they love him, they venerate him, they want to see him, to be close to him with that sort of sacred mixture of generosity and selfishness that instinctively draws people to the feet of the saints.

While the crowd demands that Padre Pio show himself as a living relic, Padre Carmelo of San Giovanni in Galdo, Father Guardian of the Convent, demands that he make a public appear-ance and therefore has decided that today the old confrere must celebrate a High Mass. Padre Carmelo has recently been nominated coordinator of the prayer groups: today is his great opportunity, and certainly he does not want the day to be diminished by any-thing happening to Padre Pio. After all, he had told him the previ-ous day, while the old friar was struggling to take in some food: "Enjoy your meal, Padre. Take courage. You must feel well. So many people have come for tomorrow's feast." But he did not consider stopping long enough to hear the response: "What feast…I should be running away for the confusion I feel."

How much is Padre Pio suffering? How much will he suffer along the *via dolorosa* of his last Mass? He too, like the agonizing Jesus, has asked the Father to take away from him the bitter chalice. And he too, like the agonizing Jesus, has chosen to obey until the end: "Oh my Jesus, my breath and my life, while I lift You today in a mystery of love, I ask You that to the world I may be for You the

Way, the Truth, and the Life. And for You may I be a holy priest, a perfect victim." He had this prayer printed on August 10, 1910, on his priestly ordination card. He never forgot it, and it is all so real today, 58 years later.

For this reason, Padre Pio chooses not to rebel to the torturers who come to him wearing the same Capuchin habit he wears. They told him that he "must feel well," and thus this morning, at 4:30 am, he has asked to be taken down to the Sacristy to prepare for the celebration. He sits down, leaning as usual with his elbows on the open drawer of the vesting cabinet, and prays, after having spent already the whole night in prayer. He then lifts his eyes and takes sight of Padre Onorato and Padre Valentino standing nearby. One of them is wearing the deacon's dalmatic, the other the tunic of the sub-deacon.

"What are you doing?" he asks, fearing what actually will be asked of him by his superior. They tell him that Father Guardian has decided that the five o'clock Mass will be a Solemn High Mass.

"Take off your vestments, because I am weak," says Padre Pio, gathering what little strength and voice he has left. At this point, Father Guardian, summoned in hurry, intervenes. There is no question: Padre Pio "must be well" and "must" celebrate a High Mass.

"But if I don't feel well…"

"It is a precept of obedience."

In the Sacristy an icy chill spreads among all who never would have wished to witness the imposition of the obligation under obedience to a suffering man destined to die before the next day's dawn. Thus, while the Padre, under obedience, lets himself be clothed with the sacred solemn vestments, Father Guardian, as described by Enrico Malatesta in *The Last Secret of Padre Pio*, explains to his astonished confreres: "The elders are like children…to obtain their obedience, sometimes one must raise his voice…Besides, what is to be done? With all these people…"

Poor victim, dazzled by lights and hymns

So, held up by the two assistants and compelled to obey, the old man walks towards the Cross. "Poor victim," writes the saint's spiritual daughter Cleonice Moncaldi in her diary *My Life Close to Padre Pio*,

> … blinded by lights and flashes, bewildered by sounds and songs! From those eyes that will no longer look at us, large tears pour out. I said to myself: "Will the last Mass be like this?". . . The Padre was absent in the literal sense of the word.[...]Where was the Padre's soul? His soul was not with us. We were not feeling his presence, or his love. My God, what is happening today?

The features of the saint, his eyes, his glance, are those of any other fearful elderly person. Anyone compassionate towards the elderly now sees one there on the altar, in the sacred appearance of Padre Pio, who celebrates High Mass imploring the hint of his assistant. Giuseppe Pagnossin, spiritual son of the stigmatic friar, will later narrate:

> All that happened on the altar during Mass was a consequence of that breath of three words: "I have no strength!" He was unable to sing the *Prefatio*: he read it; at the *Pater Noster* he started singing the *Prefatio* instead. Then he engaged all his soul and his last strength in singing the *Pater*: there is a recording of that last "song" of Padre Pio on the Cross, of that last invocation to the Father, in Latin, where one perceives the supreme effort of the soul in a sacrificial agony.

"My God, what is happening today?" How excruciating is the cry of Cleonice Morcaldi! Even more so, if one can imagine that cry coming from the lips of a pious woman at the foot of the Cross on Calvary.

Yet, where the Cross is, there is hope, even if the signs of hope are difficult to see on the dawn of this September 22, 1968. Over and over we will have to watch the tape of this Mass. We will have to caress with our eyes the sorrowful body of the Padre, and review with devout patience the photograms so we readily understand how all is coming to an end so that all can be born again.

In his intolerance, Father Guardian was indeed telling the truth when he gave the reason he had inflicted upon his holy brother the precept of obedience: "The elders are like children..." That dying old man, today, has really become again like a little child, not because of his acknowledgement of his weakness, which Father Guardian hastily mistook for a childish whim, but because of the spotlessness of the right hand, which now appears as it was before being pierced with the wound imparted by the Crucified One. The spotlessness is the sign of the innocence ready to offer itself, candid and pure, on the scaffold in the last act.

As a young priest the Padre had written to his spiritual director:

> Jesus has united me with the great bargain of human redemption. The Heavenly Father had me climb on the Cross of His Son and I am sure I will never come down from there again. I step down from the altar to get on the Cross; I come down from the Cross to lie down on the altar.

That child-like hand on an old and dying body is the sign of a destiny about to be fulfilled in its extreme act. It is a sacred stroke on a perfect painting displayed for anyone who escapes the profane nature of the crowd in order to enter into the temple of God. Fifty years earlier, that hand, along with the left hand and both feet had been visibly pierced by the same wounds of Jesus Crucified. Likewise, on August 5th of that same year, Padre Pio's side had been wounded, transfixed by a burning sword cast from the heart of Jesus. He had become the first stigmatic priest in the history of the Church.

"I unite you to my passion"

All sorts of contradictory remarks have been made about the stigmata and the stigmatic: the sign of sanctity, the abyss of lies; a man of God, a cheat and a charlatan; sacred temple, receptacle of hysteria. While the rivers of ink flowed and the people gossiped, Padre Pio was silently shedding his blood. Although the poor friar did not mention it willingly, he had been forced to describe that phenomenon in 1921, when the inquisitor Monsignor Raffaello Carlo Rossi, appointed by Rome, arrived in San Giovanni Rotondo.

Padre Pio said during one of the interrogations:

> On September 20, 1918, after celebrating Mass, while remaining in the church choir for the due thanksgiving, all of a sudden I was taken by a strong tremor, followed by a calmness, and I saw Our Lord as if He were hanging on the Cross, although I did not notice the Cross. He was lamenting the ill correspondence of men, especially the ones consecrated to Him and His more favored ones. Hence it was clear that He was suffering and that He desired to unite souls to His passion. He was inviting me to be absorbed in His sorrows and meditate on them, at the same time to care for the salvation of my brothers. After this episode I felt full of compassion for the sorrows of the Lord. While asking Him what I could do, I heard a voice saying, "I unite you to My passion." After this, the vision disappeared, and I came back to my senses. I realized that all was real, and I saw these marks here, dripping blood. I had none of them before.

Today, September 22, 1968, as all is about to be completed, these marks have disappeared: 50 years and two days after their appearance, and only 20 hours before the death of the Padre. Two pinkish eschars have fallen on the white cloth of the altar, and those hands pierced by invisible nails, after pouring out so much blood, have become immaculate once again. This episode will later be testified to by Padre Pellegrino of Sant'Elia a Pianisi, the friar in charge of being the caregiver of the Padre.

The mystery of the vanished stigmata

In his unpublished dossier, Giuseppe Pagnossin suggests a different date for the disappearance of the stigmata. To support his hypothesis, he produces two pictures he himself shot with zoom lenses from the left wing of the women's gallery of the church of San Giovanni Rotondo during the Mass celebrated by Padre Pio on September 20, 1968 on the occasion of the 50th anniversary of the apparition of his visible stigmata.

Pagnossin explains:

> Upon a first examination of the pictures, it would seem (and we would like to think that this impression corresponds to reality) that the stigmata on the back side of the right hand, as the picture shows, had disappeared. Were, then, the signs of the crucifixion already gone on the day of his last Mass, September 22, according indeed to the testimony of Padre Pellegrino, which was 48 hours before, on the anniversary of half a century of bleeding passion?

This new miracle, then, the disappearance, could have occurred two days ago, in a silence and in a seclusion far from the noise and curiosity holding sway today in this same church. It happened only the day before yesterday, and yet it seems so long ago. Perhaps it so happened because the day before yesterday, besides being precisely the 50th anniversary of the stigmata, it was also a Friday, just like that of September 20, 1918.

The mind of man is made capable of recognizing celestial patterns and designs whenever he faces God's manifestation. It would not be so bizarre if the Creator had willed to caress gently this desire for sacred embroideries within the human intelligence. If things developed according to the hypothesis of Pagnossin, those wounds, venerated and despised, which for so long had escaped human geometries, by healing after exactly 50 years in the same silence and solitude, and on the same day of the passion in which they had appeared, would prove, if there still need be a need for proof, how the Creator knows intimately His creatures and their hearts.

For his part, Padre Pio cares little about the guesswork. He had promised God he would be a victim for his brothers, and today he is completing his mission. He wrote to his spiritual director on November 29, 1910:

For a long time now, I have felt the need to offer myself to the Lord as a victim for the poor sinners and for the suffering souls in Purgatory. This desire has been growing constantly in my heart, so that it has now become what I would call a passion. I have in fact made this offering to the Lord several times, beseeching Him to pour out upon me the punishments prepared for sinners and for the souls in a state of purgation, even increasing them a hundredfold for me, as long as He converts and saves sinners and quickly admits to Paradise the souls in Purgatory. But I should now like to make this offering to the Lord in obedience to you. It seems to me that Jesus really wants this.

And now there he is, on the altar for the last time, victim in *persona Christi*, facing his own death. In pain and incapable of moving without being supported, with no strength, as he has been for a while now, he is forced to celebrate sitting down.

The final act on Calvary

Just as there was a din of voices and celestial sounds on Calvary 2,000 years ago, here too, there is a clash of the ordinary multitude and of heavenly talk around the altar: there are the confreres who address each other to accommodate the Padre: "Hey you there, come here, careful, careful, careful." Then there is the Padre, who, exhausted, repeats what the deacon prompts him to say: *Orate fratres*: *ut meum ac vestrum sacrificium...*, and so on until the end. To a first *Dominus vobiscum*, a second *Dominus vobiscum* follows; to the one *Benedicat vos*, a second *Benedicat vos* echoes; to the initial *omnipotens Deus*, the corresponding one follows: *omnipotens Deus*. These are echoes the microphones capture until the *Pater, et Filius, et Spiritus Sanctus*.

Ite missa est. The organ again takes control of the church, while the friars help the saint stand up to return to the sacristy: "This way. Straight ahead. Turn, turn, turn." The choir begins singing. "Watch out, Padre!" Choir and organ break up in a choked cry when the Padre is about to fall, stricken by heart failure. Friar Giuseppe Pio, known as Friar Bill, manages to grab and support him, until they bring in the wheelchair from the sacristy: an authentic deposition.

The poor victim shows a tremor of life while they carry him away, passing through the crowd: "My children…my children," he manages to say. Is he perhaps seeing again the night between August 9 and 10, 1910, the night before his ordination, when he was lifted to the light of Heaven to know the souls that God had predestined to his care? Back then, He saw them all, even the ones of his spiritual children not yet born. He assumed them all into his priesthood with the duty to answer for them, expiate, enlighten, love, and lead them one day to Heaven. Could he perhaps be seeing all of them now also?

Pagnossin recounts an unknown detail underlining the extreme sacrificial character of those emotional moments: "Mr. Giovanni Scarparo of Montagnana, who had attended the Padre's Mass from the women's gallery, came down and stood on the first section of the corridor between the new and the old sacristy. He had in his hands a recording device. Next to him were Padre Clemente of Santa Maria in Punta and Padre Benigno of Sant'Ilario Milanese (former Superior General of the Capuchins). Let us follow the taped conversation that took place:

> Padre Paolo: "Now, go upstairs, Padre Pio…"
> Padre Onorato to Padre Pio: "Would you like to give confessions for a little while?"
> Padre Pio: "I'll do what you wish."
> Padre Onorato to Padre Pio: "Are you not feeling well?"
> Padre Pio motions that he does not.
> An unknown voice: "No, he cannot."
> Padre Onorato to Padre Pio: "You tell me, Spiritual Father, as you like … Here is the Most Reverend one. He desires to wish you *prosit* [to give you his best wishes]. Here is this other Most Reverend one, who is the former Superior General."

Padre Benigno out loud: "*Prosit.*"
Padre Pio: "Uh! Scream a little louder!"[1]

The conversation continues a little longer. Then the voice of Mr. Scarparo is heard recommending his daughter Claudia to the Padre.

It is impossible not to notice the sentence, "I'll do what you wish," in response to the question if he would like to give confessions, or that motion of denial when asked if he would be able to. Signs of obedience carried up to the extreme point of duty, a line of the Divine Office of a dying man who can offer nothing else but his submission to whomever represents authority.

"I also screamed in sorrow when I saw the Padre fainting. I screamed aloud," wrote Cleonice Morcaldi afterwards in her diary.

> On my way home, with my soul shaken, I thought: "Could this be his last Mass?" But the Padre had told me that he would die on the altar: of love and pain, and that his last glance would be to his brothers in exile. This glance, yes, was directed to everyone, but he did not die! But then, how could he have died among such a crowd? What would have happened? A pandemonium! What would the Carabinieri [Italian elite police] have done? I think that the sweet victim, while looking persistently at the Carabiniere next to him, was thinking about all this, and, making one last sacrifice to God, he prayed that his death be postponed to the following night, in solitude and silence, and on another altar: on the chair where he used to wake and suffer, where he used to wake and pray, and where, like Moses on the mountain, he used to lift his arms to God, to hold back His arm rightly outraged by sinners. God granted his request.

The last farewell. Now the Padre goes to die.

The Padre is now in his cell. He recovers a little and would like to go down to hear confessions, but Padre Onorato is able to dissuade him. He rests as much as he can during the day, then, at six

---

[1] This is said with an ironic tone, referring to the fact that they wanted to be heard on television.

o'clock in the afternoon, shows up in the women's gallery to join the evening prayers. While approaching his cell in exhaustion, he tries to bless his spiritual children, but he does not even have the strength to lift his right hand. Once again Padre Onorato, understanding his desire, holds up his right arm and helps him to trace the sign of the cross. Then, while escorted to his cell, he looks out of a window in the corridor and greets all for the last time, waving a white handkerchief. "Good night, Padre," they say from below. "We love you so much." "Thank you for everything Padre." "Have a good rest, Padre."

But now, the Padre goes to die. During that night, in the adjacent cell is Padre Pellegrino. He will be the nurse on duty. This evening the Padre is restless; he calls for him several times. At ten past midnight: "Young man, did you offer Mass?" "It is too early," Padre Pellegrino answers. "It is only midnight." "Oh well, this morning you will offer Mass for me."

At half past midnight, he asks to receive Confession. Afterwards he says: "If the Lord calls me today, ask forgiveness of the brothers for the bother I gave them and ask my confreres and my spiritual children for a prayer for my soul." Padre Pellegrino is uneasy and tries somehow to be light, but he cannot refrain from adding: "If you were to be right, can I ask you for one last blessing for the confreres, the spiritual children, for your sick people?" "Yes, I bless them all. Only, I beg the Superior for the charity that he himself may give this blessing on my behalf."

But what really strikes the nurse-friar is the Padre's desire to renew his religious vows. The young friar starts reciting that sacred formula and the dying saint follows along repeating slowly, sentence after sentence, word by word, the great promise to the Lord, until Padre Pellegrino concludes: "And I, on God's behalf, if you will observe all of this, I promise to you eternal life."

"What time is it?" Now the Padre seems to have no other care than to know what time of the night it is, "as if he had an appointment," the nurse-friar reflects. Then, at 1:00 am, he asks to get up, rinses his face, combs his hair, and, reciting the rosary, walks towards the balcony: as a faithful servant he knows he has to work in the Lord's vineyard until the last moment. So much harvest to lead to the Lord is out there, and there is no time to waste. Padre Pellegrino perceives in the rhythm of the prayer the names of Jesus and Mary, the two names of eternal salvation.

The Padre is now again in his cell. "Tell me, who is there?" Padre Pellegrino answers: "There is the picture of your mother." "I see two mothers." And he does not accept any reasonable answer. "I see there two mothers." His assistant will relate later: "I thought then that this could be something out of the ordinary and wished to insist, but he started saying: 'Jesus, Mary, Jesus, Mary...' and he no longer answered me."

The strange disheartening of the friars

It is clear at this point that all is about to be accomplished. The Padre rapidly gets worse. Padre Pellegrino gets worried, but the dying saint tells him not to disturb anyone. "Spiritual Father, I am sorry, but you are not in charge now, I am." Some confreres arrive first, then the doctor, Dr. Giuseppe Sala. Then the Father Guardian is informed, and Dr. Giuseppe Gusso and Dr. Giovanni Scarale of the Casa Sollievo della Sofferenza are summoned. Padre Paolo of San Giovanni Rotondo administers Extreme Unction. Medical care can do nothing else because it is now 2:31 am on September 23, 1968, the hour Our Lord had established for Padre Pio to go back to his home, cleaned of any wound, with the habit of St. Francis covering his body, immaculate like that of a child. Jesus crucified took back His stigmata.

But the trials of the Padre are not over yet. Giuseppe Pagnossin says in his dossier:

> It is still inexplicable today, looking back at the account of that dawn when the saint entered "his glory," how the friars could be disheartened by an event that should have filled with saintly joy the souls of the witnesses, and, if divulged like an *Alleluia*, also of all the Catholic souls in the world: the disappear-

ance of the stigmata, the sudden healing of those wounds that had been pouring for 50 years a river of blood for the atonement of the sins of all of us. It was indeed a prodigy as significant as that of their sudden appearance, ultimately a proof of their supernatural origin.

How did it happen that some of the Capuchins panicked to the point that the Father Guardian Carmelo of San Giovanni in Galdo and, of course, the apostolic administrator Padre Clemente of Santa Maria in Punta, found it opportune to order that the body of Padre Pio be exposed to the faithful wearing the half gloves on his hands, just as the stigmatic friar had done in modesty for 50 years? Who cannot see that would have been, after all, an act of "justice and truth," to display to public veneration the body of Padre Pio "healed," by the will of God, from all infirmities, in the same way his elect soul had already appeared free from any suffering in front of the throne of his Lord? The faithful from every part of the world and the "generous inhabitants of San Giovanni Rotondo" were discussing this in front of the body lying in state.

A "perfect" cycle, unique in the history of the Church, had come to a close—exactly 50 years of visible stigmata—and the world was kept in the dark regarding such an event that represented the conclusive, shining confirmation of a charismatic gift from Divine Providence to His good and faithful servant. What is taking place in front of Padre Pio's body now that he is dead? The apostolic administrator seems only concerned that the absence of the stigmata remain a secret and, from now on, everyone in the convent is bound to this decision. Padre Ferdinando of Riese, biographer of the saint, will say that this is an act of prudence aimed at preventing "mistaken and rushed interpretations." In other words, in front of the body of the Padre, instead of praising God for the new miracle, they are worried that someone may cry out "fraud." So, this means that here too, inside the convent, they worry that that old man who just died may have been an impostor.

In the sacrifice that Padre Pio had offered a few hours earlier, he had laid himself on the altar for the last time, carrying nailed in his heart the terrible awareness of being considered a liar by too many of his own brothers.

The knight of the Faith

Even so, despite the humiliations, the adversities, the sufferings, and the torments, this man whom the Church will declare a saint gave justice to the fidelity of God until the end. He had done this on the altar and then in his cell, where he returned his soul to the Creator who conceived him and loved him from eternity. He did the same also in his last hours, with the certainty that what is beyond hope, what is humanly absurd, manifests itself quickly already in this life. But one must have faith to notice it.

On mount Moriah, Abraham lived the marvel of such certainty up to its immense climax. His Lord had put him to the test by asking for the sacrifice of his son, and all he could do was to obey and, at the same time, surrender in faith: to venture into the absurd to save the life of Isaac and his own soul. Kierkegaard, in *Fear and Trembling*, gives a detailed account of this:

> Nonetheless Abraham believed and believed for this life. Certainly, if his faith was only for a future reality, then it would have been easy for him to rush to exit this world where he did not belong. But such was not the faith of Abraham, if there ever be such a faith; for deep down this is not faith but the furthest possibility of faith[. . .]. But Abraham believed precisely for this life, that he was to grow old in that land, honored by the people, blessed in his posterity, unforgettable in Isaac[. . .]. Abraham believed and did not doubt, he believed in the absurd.[2]

Padre Pio lived all his life on the edge of what human frivolities call absurd. He did this up to the last Mass he celebrated in an

---

[2] Søren Kierkegaard, "A Panegyric Upon Abraham" in *Fear and Trembling*, 1843 (translated by Walter Lowrie, Princeton University Press, 1941, pp. 25-26). *Editor's Note:* The use of Kierkegaard—a Lutheran existentialist philosopher—in the text should not be taken as a full endorsement of his theological or philosophical works.

excruciating obedience. He did it also while death was visiting him, by reading the doubt in the minds of so many confreres incredulous in front of the miracle of the vanished stigmata. But, precisely now that he is gone, it is much more evident that this friar, beaten in his body and soul, is what Kierkegaard calls the "knight of the faith." He is the one able to accomplish the motion of the infinite whereby he renounces in perfect humility all he owns in the world. But, immediately after, he plunges back into the finite by savoring human things with the same intensity of one who has never known anything more sublime. He is the one who embodies the paradox of faith whereby one gives up everything certain to gain a hundred fold in this life and eternity:

> It suffices the simple human courage to give up all the temporal reality in the hope to gain eternity[…]. It is needed instead a humble courage to be able to grasp all of the temporal reality using the absurd and this is the courage of the faith. By faith Abraham did not give up Isaac, by faith Abraham obtained Isaac.

The infinite and finite actions of the Padre are the ones of a mystic who first offers himself to the designs of human tantrums and wickedness to find later the votive order of the ecstatic gaze or of a healed wound.

In these last hours, as he was approaching his death, the movement of the infinite manifested itself in the harsh and painful loneliness spent in obeying the last cruel orders. And the movement of the finite focused in the vivacity of the eyes gazing at the elevated host during Mass and in the childlike purity regained by his flesh wounded for 50 years.

Like St. Francis

Now that the Padre is dead, the memory goes to the portrait of St. Francis by Francisco de Zurbarán. That man standing up, with his head covered by the hood, his hands hidden inside the sleeves of the habit and his glance towards our Lord, does not represent the saint as if he were living, but his incorrupt body after his death, as he was found incorrupt in the crypt in Assisi.

Usually, the finding of Francis is depicted as a narrated episode. Zurbarán, with inspired geniality, preferred to codify it in celestial stillness in the same way as the celebrant does with the rubrics of the missal. That is why he depicts the saint all alone; standing like a sculpture carved by the light while he mysteriously emerges from a dense darkness. Only the face, half hidden by the shade, looks to be made of flesh. His eye, brightened by love, points towards Heaven. All leads to witness the bodily manifestation of someone coming back from the world of the dead. It is an epiphany lacking terrifying notes because the soul is full of supernatural serenity and beatitude.

And now, in San Giovanni Rotondo, another St. Francis is stretched on his death bed worthy of another Zurbarán.

CHAPTER 2

The Temple of God
and the Smoke of Satan

Padre Pio explains how during the divine sacrifice he
follows Jesus up to the Cross, while too many Christians
prefer the snares of the world

While Padre Pio was dying, down there, at the feet of Calvary
outlined among the Gargano Mountains, the Italy of the economic
boom was basking in its small achievements in the illusion that
they would last forever. They were the last steps of the dance of
a society inebriated by the very secular "economic miracle"[1] and
unaware of the tunnel of hate and lead that it would be entering
in the years to come.

The Padre had offered his last sacrifice at the time when that
"miracle" was beginning to show all its contradictory weaknesses:
Azzurro, The Doll, The Rain Falls, "*Killing a Fascist is not a Crime,*"
Canzonissima, The Black Arrow, The Pickwick Papers, "*Viva Marx,
Viva Lenin, Viva Mao-Tse-Tung,*" *2001: A Space Odyssey, Bandits
in Milan, The Family Doctor,* and "*Hard Fight with No Fear.*"[2] It
was the year 1968, a year destined to pass into history written in
capital letters: "Sixty-Eight" ["'68"]—as are all years which sym-

---

[1] The economic growth experienced by Italy in the decade 1955-1965 was called
the "economic miracle."

[2] This is a list of popular songs, TV shows, and movies of the time. *Viva* = "long
live." Those enclosed within quotations are slogans shouted during political dem-
onstrations at that time.

37

bolize revolutions: "Eighty-Nine" ["'89"], "Forty-Eight" ["'48,"] and "Seventeen" ["'17"]. [3]

Those times, a little careless and a little sad, pictured in black and white on the TV screen, had reached the end of the line. The newspapers would soon start talking of the students' rebellion, of violence and permanent revolution, of hate for any form of authority and for any symbol of it, of the irrepressible search for any form of liberation. They would speak well of those things, of course; because of conviction, or conformism, or anger, or cowardice. Or, perhaps simply, they would do it because it was generally felt that the "68" had started, a year which would voraciously swallow all the neighboring ones, the years preceding and those following it.

Among the first of those to venture into that tunnel as vanguard of the revolution were many Catholics. The first skirmishes had left no doubt. On February 15, 1966, the Colombian priest Camilo Torres had died during a guerrilla attack. He would later become one of the symbols of the Catholic revolt inside and outside the Church. In that same year, on October 9, Cardinal Bernard Jan Alfrink presented in Utrecht the *New Dutch Catechism,* which openly questioned Catholic teachings on sin, redemption, the Eucharist, the virginity of Mary Mother of God, the role of the Church and of the pope. On October 10, 1967, during the third World Congress for the Lay Apostolate, held in Rome, the delegates officially commemorated the guerrilla Ernesto Che Guevara, killed the day before by the regular Bolivian army. On November 17, 1967, began the first occupation of the Catholic University of the Sacred Heart in Milan.

The "Catholic 68,"[4] to which journalist Roberto Beretta dedicated the essay *The Long Autumn,* and from which some of the citations in this chapter have been taken, arrived from various sources but would have great effects. And, if the virulence used by its militants in systematically reversing orthodoxy is astounding,

---

[3] The years are: 1789, 1848, 1917. The abbreviated form, using only the last two digits, would be commonly understood in Italy.

[4] Again, this is a common abbreviation in Italy for 1968.

even more astounding is the number of those who had the duty, the authority, and the power to stop the militants but did nothing or almost nothing to counter it. Occupations of cathedrals, interruptions of religious ceremonies with staging of alternative rituals, open protest against the bishops and the pope, systematic refusal of the formation programs in the seminaries, communities under the guidance of priests opposing ecclesiastic authority, pastors and bishops blessing all types of protest, profanation of the Eucharist with rites and prayers invented *ex novo* [from scratch], alternative masses improvised according to the "local genius." These are all facts to which we can link the names of many people and many places.

Meanwhile, a stigmatic Capuchin, down in the land of Gargano, continued offering the Divine Sacrifice in atonement for the scars inflicted by men to the face of God.

Padre Pio had told his spiritual daughter Cleonice Morcaldi what that sacrifice meant to him. This dialogue is dense with doctrine and devotion, a little treatise of Catholic theology of the Mass, a mystic gem through which a man of God humbly accepts that anyone may probe deeply inside his sanctity. It was published by Giuseppe Pagnossin in his dossier; it was then sectioned and studied to find out what was "the Mass of Padre Pio."

Some commented on this treatise with theological subtlety, step by step, showing its depths and peaks along which the soul and body of the stigmatic friar ran; the speaker, all the while, remains nailed on the altar. Yet it is possible to give homage to the purity of that treasure of faith by using it as a measure and a comparison to what men think and do when they abandon the right paths leading to God.

The treatise may also be examined by simply inserting in the dialogue between Padre Pio and Cleonice Morcaldi, various paragraphs, episodes, and memories from the "Catholic 68." This would perhaps be a technique more apt to television than to literature, but substantially effective in showing in writing the fleeting nature of the rebellion against the rights of God and against the inalterability of sacred obedience.

How aged now seem the reasons, the motives, and the illusions of those rebels who deluded themselves into being eternal only because they were young! And how exquisitely fresh remain instead the words of the old Padre Pio! The farmers of the Italian countryside used to say: "Better an old man singing than a young man in the field tilling." The truth of this is even more profound when the old man, like the Friar of the Gargano, speaks about Paradise, whereas the young man, like the rebels of the "Catholic 68," talk only about earth. This truth glares mercilessly before the reader's eyes in the following pages, where the technique of television editing produces a peculiar effect: while Padre Pio's words effectively morph into living images of color and vitality, the slogans of the rebels flow into a melancholic and deadening black and white.

Q. *Padre, what is your Mass?*
A. A sacred union with the passion of Jesus.
Q. *What should I gather from your Holy Mass?*
A. The whole of Calvary.
Q. *Padre, tell me all that you suffer during Holy Mass.*
A. All that Jesus suffered in His passion; inadequately I suffer too, to the extent that it is possible for a human creature. It all happens despite all my faults and only because of His goodness.
Q. *Padre, how can we get to know your passion?*
A. By knowing the passion of Jesus; in the passion of Jesus you will find mine too.
Q. *Do you agonize, Padre, like Jesus in the Garden?*
A. Sure.
Q. *Does the Angel come to comfort you, like he did to Jesus?*
A. Yes.
Q. *Which one is your* fiat?
A. To suffer and always suffer for my brothers in this exile and for His Divine Reign.

It was with the advent of liberation theology in the early 70s that was revealed to us the evangelical truth whereby all those who fight for the poor, believers or atheists, would be united after death; and the kingdom of God, or kingdom of Heaven, and the perfect communist society are one and the same thing; and believing in immortality, as said in my country by José Coronel Urtecho, means that the revolution does not end in this world. It was actually right here in Cuba, during my first visit, that I discovered how the French Jesuit Father de Lubac had transformed St. Augustine's saying "Love and do what you will" into "Love and believe what you will." [...] And then there was the entrance of Fidel in Havana: an apotheosis. [...] Those days were like the final judgment because everyone was given what he deserved: to some punishments, to others rewards. And all that was hidden came to light: good and bad. Fidel had a clearer idea of Christianity than most bishops. He said that the Cuban clergy, ally of the rich, had prostituted the essence of primitive Christianity.

(Father Ernesto Cardenal, Trappist monk and Minister of Culture in the Nicaraguan junta)

Q. *You have said too: "They will shout:* 'Crucifige! Crucifige!'" *Who will be shouting?*
A. The sons of men, the very recipients of the benefits.

The Word of God was not given only to you, but to the whole people of God; you are not the owner, but the servant; you are not the judge, but the judged. Yours is an opinion. [...] You do not share in the poverty of the people of God. As long as you will remain isolated in your privileged position you will be unable to understand both your brothers and the Word of God.

(Open letter by the assembly of ecclesial protest of the Catholic University of Milan to Cardinal Giovanni Colombo for Lent 1969)

"Florit, we know only your photograph. Without communion with the people you are no longer a bishop."
"Bishop, either retract your words or resign."

"A father does not go against his children."

(*Banners by the protesters of the Florentine
Community of the Isolotto against Cardinal Ermenegildo
Florit, Archbishop of Florence, October 1968*)

Q. *How was Jesus after the scourging?*
A. The Prophet says it: "He became one whole wound; He became like a leper."
Q. *Then you, too, are one whole wound, from head to toe?*
A. Is this not our glory? And if there will be no more room on my body for more wounds, we will lay wound upon wound.
Q *My God, this is too much! You are, Padre, a real torturer of yourself!*
A. Do not fear, but rejoice. I do not desire suffering *per se*, no; but for the fruit it gives me. Suffering gives glory to God and saves my brothers, what else can I ask for?

> [....] The Revolution is not only legitimate, it is obligatory for the Christians who see in it the only effective and complete method to bring about universal love. [...] I left the privileges and duty of clergy, but I never stopped being a priest. I believe I dedicated myself to the Revolution for love of neighbor. I stopped saying Mass to bring about that love of neighbor in the secular, economic, and social realm. When my neighbor will have nothing against me, when the Revolution will be accomplished, I will again say Mass, if God will let me. I believe this is the way to follow Christ's mandate: "If therefore thou offer thy gift at the altar, and there thou remember that thy brother hath any thing against thee; leave there thy offering before the altar, and go first to be reconciled to thy brother: and then coming thou shalt offer thy gift" (Mt. 5:23-24). After the Revolution, we Christians will have the awareness of having installed a system oriented toward love of neighbor. The struggle is long, let us begin now...

(*Camillo Torres, Colombian guerrilla priest, killed in 1966*)

Q. *Padre, when at night you get scourged, are you by yourself or is someone assisting you?*
A. The Holy Virgin assists me; the whole Heaven is present.
Q. *Jesus made me feel that you suffer the crown of thorns. Is it true?*
A. The immolation would not be complete otherwise.
Q. *Which sins did Jesus expiate with the crown of thorns?*
A. All of them. Especially the sins of thoughts, not excluding the meaningless and useless ones.

Bouquet of reactions to the encyclical *Humanae Vitae* of Pope Paul VI, 1968:

We notice with surprise that the encyclical does not correspond to the expectations aroused by the pastoral constitution *Gaudium et Spes.* (*Dutch theologians*)

The married couple can decide responsibly according to their conscience that artificial contraception in some circumstances is allowed and indeed necessary to preserve and augment the value and sacramental meaning of marriage. (*Theologians of the Catholic University of America in Washington, D.C.*)

The Holy Father in his letter does not speak of grave sin. If anyone contravenes the teaching of the encyclical, he should in no way consider himself separated from the love of God and can receive communion without confession. (*Austrian Episcopal Conference*)

The unity of the Church does not consist of the mere uniformity on all points, but rather in the unity of faith and heart, in the humble, loyal search for truth. (*Canadian Episcopal Conference*)

We cannot adhere to the request for obedience to the papal teaching. (*Declaration of the 82nd Catholic Day in Essen, Germany*)

Q. *The thorns, Padre, do you have them on your forehead or all around your head?*

A. All around my head.

Q. *Padre, how many thorns are there in your crown?...30?*

A. Oh yeah!

Q. *Padre, I think that your crown is made of not 30, but 300 thorns.*

A. You get dumbfounded by a zero digit! Is it not then 30 contained in 300?

Q. *Padre, is it true that during Mass you suffer the torture of the crowning of thorns?*

A. Do you have any doubt?

Q. *Is it during the whole duration of the Mass?*

A. And before and after. You must never let go of the diadem.

Q. *Padre, do you also suffer what Jesus suffered on the way to Calvary?*

A. I do, yes, but there is so much more before reaching what the Divine Master suffered!

Q. *Who are for you the Cyrenean and Veronica?*

A. Jesus Himself.

Q. *In the divine sacrifice, Padre, do you take upon yourself our iniquities?*

A. It could not be otherwise, because this is part of the divine sacrifice.

Q. *Our Lord then thinks of you as a sinner?*

A. I don't know, but I fear I am.

There cannot be Revelation without revolution. We Christians who live and remain in the Church must be its negation; we who love the Church to the point of martyrdom must demystify and destroy whatever pagan is in Her to re-create a Community that shares the faith and does not separate in its name, a community of makers of justice, a community of revolutionaries for the world of the poor and the oppressed.

(Paolo Sobri, explaining why, on March 26, 1968, he interrupted the homily in Trent's cathedral and continued with a contra-Lent on the church plaza)[5]

Q. *I saw you trembling while climbing the stairs of the altar. Why? Is it because of what you are going to suffer?*

A. Not because of what I am going to suffer, but because of what I am going to offer.

Q. *Which are the hours of the day, Padre, when you suffer much?*

A. During the celebration of the Holy Mass.

Q. *Do you suffer also during the day, Padre, the same way you suffer during Holy Mass?*

A. Poor me! How could I work? How could I exercise my Ministry?

Q. *During what part of the Divine Sacrifice do you suffer most?*

A. Always and to an ever increasing degree.

Q. *In celebrating Holy Mass, at which moment do you suffer most?*

A. From Consecration to Communion.

Q. *During what part of the Mass do you suffer the scourging?*

A. From the beginning to the end, but more intensely after Consecration.

Q. *Why do you cry almost every time, Padre, when reading the Gospel during Holy Mass?*

A. Does it seem to you a little matter that God converses with His creatures? And to be contradicted by them? And to be continuously wounded by their ingratitude and incredulity?

> For us the great news of Christmas is the death of God. That God does not exist: He has been invented by men to explain the mysteries of nature, of the "established" order, and of evil. [...] It goes without saying that the next world does not exist. All

---

[5] Paolo Sorbi, professor of sociology, is a former Marxist, former member of the Italian Communist party, and convert to Catholicism. He currently heads up the Pro-Life office of the Archdiocese of Milan, and is the program manager of the Italian Catholic radio station, Radio Maria (as reported in www.catholic.org on 11/25/2012)].

the inventions of theologians about Heaven, Hell, Purgatory are obviously but fantasies. The only reality that exists is human.

(*Christmas message of the school chaplains of the Vandée, 1968*)

Q. *Is your Mass, Padre, a bloody sacrifice?*
A. You heretic!
Q. *No. I mean to say that the one of Jesus is bloodless; but your participation to all the Passion is bloody. Am I wrong?*
A. Well! . . . You are not wrong there. Looking at it from a personal standpoint, you may be right.
Q. *Who wipes your blood during Mass?*
A. Nobody.
Q. *Why do you cry at the Offertory?*
A. Are you trying to snatch my secret? So be it. That is the point when the soul gets detached from the profane.
Q. *During your Mass, Padre, the crowd gets a little noisy!*
A. What if you had been on Calvary, where you could hear screams, curses, noises, threats!? It was all a racket there.
Q. *Do the noises in church distract you?*
A. Not at all.

The general strike in protest against the structural injustice of the world is the true contemporary liturgy of Easter.

(*Fr. Jean Cardonnel, at the Congress Gospel and Revolution, held in Paris in the occasion of Lent 1968*)

Q. *Padre, are all the souls who participate in your Mass present to your spirit?*
A. I see all my children at the altar, as if in a mirror.
Q. *Tell me why you suffer so much at the Consecration.*
A. Because it is right there that a new and admirable destruction and creation takes place. You cannot unveil the secrets of the High King without desecrating them. You ask me why I suffer? I wish I could pour not just little tears, but streams of tears!

Can't you ponder the terrific mystery? A God who is victim of our sins! We are moreover his butchers.

> The church of a big city. No sacred sign, but for a cross in the background. [...] In the so-called presbytery, a dark wooden table with no cloth; on it a big glass, a flask-like bottle filled with red wine, a wooden basket filled with flat round bread. [...] From the back progresses a young man in brown and the celebrant wearing a long mantle open in the front, with wide sleeves. Having said a prayer, he sits among the faithful in a small chair in the first row. The young man who accompanied him reads the Epistle and the Gospel, and gives a homily. He also is a priest. Then the presider of the assembly goes to the table, opens the bottle, pours the wine into the glass, dries his hands with a handkerchief taken from his jacket under the mantle, and the Eucharistic celebration starts. At Communion, the priest in lay clothing arrives carrying another tray, takes half of the bread pieces, and then he and the celebrant advance toward the assembly. Everyone, as in all churches, takes communion.
>
> (Dom Luigi Rosadoni, from "The Dutch Catholics," That Is the Risk of Living, 1968)

Q. *Do you suffer, Padre, the bitterness of the bile?*
A. Yes, and often, often.
Q. *Padre, how can you keep yourself standing at the altar?*
A. The same way that Jesus held Himself up at Calvary.
Q. *At the altar, are you suspended on the Cross like Jesus at Calvary?*
A. Do you even bother asking that?
Q. *And how do you hold yourself up?*
A. Just like Jesus did on Calvary.
Q. *Did the executioners turn the Cross upside down to clinch the nails?*
A. It goes without saying!
Q. *Do they clinch your nails too?*
A. Oh yes!
Q. *Do they turn over your Cross as well?*

A. Yes, but don't be afraid.

Q. *Padre, do you also recite during Mass the seven words that Jesus uttered on the Cross?*

A. Yes, unworthily, I recite them too.

Q. *To whom do you say "Woman, here is your son"?*

A. I tell Her: Here are the sons of your Son.

Q. *Do you suffer the same thirst and abandonment as Jesus?*

A. Yes.

Q. *In which moment do you suffer the thirst and abandonment?*

A. After Consecration.

Q. *Until when do you suffer thirst and abandonment?*

A. Usually until Communion.

Q. *Did Jesus crucified consume nourishment? What was the crucified Jesus thirsty of?*

A. Of the reign of God.

> Che Guevara, for example, had also a messianic aspect, somewhat reminiscent of our Christian formation. It is true, we have sympathized for the socialist revolutions in the Third World: Allende's Chile, Cuba, the Nicaragua of the Sandinistas. But why? Because we wanted to bring about Marxism? No, we did not give a damn. We wanted to realize the Gospel, the Gospel of the poor. If, confronted with the Gospel, you follow your heart, it is inevitable not to sympathize with this reality.
>
> *(Dom Enzo Mazzi, leader of the*
> *Isolotto Community of Florence)*

Q. *You told me that you are ashamed to say: "In vain I looked for one who would comfort me."[6] Why?*

A. Because compared to what Jesus suffered, we, the truly guilty ones, turn pale.

Q. *In front of whom are you ashamed?*

A. In front of God and my conscience.

---

[6] Ps. 68:21

It was toward the end of the Council and those were the days when the psychological impossibility was emerging for Pope Montini to proceed audaciously on the road to collegiality. That evening, ours was a good get-together, as an important foreign Jesuit was talking to us very coldly of the vital problems; Father Davide [Turoldo] reached us, later, as he did habitually, since he did not tolerate missing gatherings of friends, even if they occurred at the same time. He sat in silence, but it was clear that inside he was stirred by a multitude of sentiments. And when the Jesuit mentioned Paul VI, Davide jumped up, opened his huge arms and roared: "We must kill this pope!" The Jesuit looked at the clock and said, terrified: "It is late, I must go..."

(Ettore Masina, political journalist, founder with Paul Gauthier of the network Radié Resch)[7]

Q. *Do the angels of God comfort you on the altar where you immolate yourself?*
A. Well...I do not detect them.
Q. *If solace does not descend into your spirit during the divine sacrifice, and you, like Jesus, suffer in a total abandonment, is our presence useless?*
A. The benefit is for you. Should we then call useless the presence of the Sorrowful Mother, John, and the pious women at the feet of the dying Jesus!
Q. *Padre, why don't you give us, too, a little of this passion of yours?*
A. The Bridegroom's jewels cannot be donated to anyone.
Q. *Tell me then what can I do to lighten up your Calvary.*
A. Lighten up?...You should rather ask to make it heavier, we must suffer!
Q. *It is painful to witness your martyrdom and be unable to help you!*

---

[7] Masina was considered an expert on Vatican affairs, and was elected to the Italian House of Representatives as a member of the Italian Communist Party, all the while apparently calling himself a Catholic. Paul Gauthier was a French priest, a promoter of the idea of the worker-priest who worked as a carpenter among the Palestinian poor.

A. The Sorrowful Mother, too, had to witness. It was certainly more comforting to Jesus to have a Sorrowful Mother, rather than an indifferent one.

Q. *What was the Virgin doing at the feet of Jesus crucified?*

A. She was suffering, seeing her son suffer. She offered her sorrows and the pains of Jesus to the Heavenly Father for our salvation.

Q. *Not for the sake of curiosity, but I ask you which one of your wounds makes you suffer the most?*

A. The head and the heart.

Q. *What is Holy Communion?*

A. It is totally an interior and exterior mercy. It is an embrace. Go ahead and pray Jesus that He may be felt sensibly by you.

> Some among us have been sharing for some years the bread and the wine, sometimes bitter, of the struggle for justice. [...] It has been a few weeks now that we shared also the bread and wine of the fight, even on the street, within the deep movement that wants to reject a malformed society. We are living in an immense hope, such that perhaps, at least the younger ones of us, have never experienced. We thought it impossible, at the moment of thanksgiving, to go back home, each to his own house. Let each one ponder in his conscience whether he can participate in this action in full truth. If anyone among us cannot do it, he will show it by abstaining from communion and all will respect this decision.
>
> After the Bible readings and the consecration formula recited collectively, the philosopher Paul Ricoeur comments: "Above all, we must remember that without students and without workers we would not be together here today. They have made this revolutionary action possible for us. Thus, they are present with us now, like these loaves of bread and this wine."
>
> *(Pentecost 1968, Ecumenical Eucharist*
> *of Rue de Vaugirard, Paris)*

Q. *Where does Jesus kiss you?*

A. He kisses me everywhere.

Q. *When Jesus comes, does He visit only your soul?*
A. He visits my whole being.
Q. *What does Jesus do at Communion?*
A. He delights in His creature.
Q. *Is Communion an embodiment?*
A. It is a fusion. The same as when two candles melted together are no longer distinct from each other.
Q. *When you are united with Jesus in Communion, what should we ask Our Lord for you?*
A. That I may be another Jesus, all Jesus, always Jesus.

> We do not want to be friars minor, because we do not know what it means to be a friars minor. We want to be religious atheists. Yes, and willingly, if in the sense that we want to cease to be the professionals or the professors of God. Our "religious order" is for us something extremely secondary, because our "order" is mankind.
>
> (*Letter of eleven Franciscan novices of Milan to their superior, Spring 1968*

Q. *You made me understand that the holy species do not get consumed in you; that the blood of Jesus flows in your veins; are you then a living monstrance?*
A. You said it!
Q. *Why do you cry, Padre, when you take Communion?*
A. If the Church cries out: "You did not disdain the womb of the Virgin," referring to the Incarnation, what should be said about us, miserable ones?!
Q. *Do you suffer also at Communion?*
A. That is the apex.
Q. *After Communion, do your sufferings continue?*
A. Yes, but as loving sufferings.
Q. *In this union, does Jesus console you?*
A. Yes, but He never ceases hanging on the Cross.
Q. *To whom did the dying Jesus turn His last glance?*
A. To His Mother.

Q. *And you, to whom do you turn it?*
A. To my brothers in this exile.

> Is it still licit to be Catholics? It is the Pacellian Church that is
> not Catholic?[8] Will it never be obedient again? The schism exists,
> now it must be declared. Better an anti-pope than the putre-
> faction of religious experience. The ignorant, the sanfedisti,[9]
> the clericals, and the reactionaries can keep the Church of
> Bellarmine[10] and Pacelli. Let the new Catholics make a schism.
> And you, the few in the high hierarchy who have our trust: you,
> the Alfrinks, the Suenenses, the Dopfners, the Pellegrinos, and
> the Helder Camaras, the time for prudence is over. Count your
> followers and, however many they may be, get out of the Church
> that does not deserve you any more, if it is true that you have
> not deceived us. The new Catholicism has already been born.

(Il Confronto, *a Milanese periodical, October 1968*)

Q. *You too die during Holy Mass?*
A. Mystically in the Holy Communion.
Q. *Is it by fervor of love or of sorrow that you die?*
A. For both.
Q. *At Communion you undergo death: are you no longer on the
altar then?*
A. Why? Even the dead Jesus was on Calvary.
Q. *You said, Padre, that at Communion the Victim dies. Do they
lay you in the arms of the Blessed Mother?*
A. In the arms of St. Francis.
Q. *Padre, does Jesus detach His arms from the Cross to rest in you?*
A. It is I who rest in Him.
Q. *How much do you love Jesus?*
A. The desire to love Him is infinite, but, in practice—alas!—I
would say, zero, and I am ashamed of it.

---

[8] Eugenio Pacelli was Pope Pius XII.
[9] Sanfedisti (soldiers of the Holy Faith) generally refers to any popular uprising in
support of the Catholic religion. The original movement took place in the Kingdom of Naples against sympathizers of the French Revolution.
[10] St. Robert Bellarmine, Cardinal and Doctor of the Church, 1542-1621.

There is a useful protest, beyond the brutal and anarchic form. Beyond many impurities that we must refuse and we reject, we must rejoice in the deep demands of which we recognize the human values that are profoundly Christian: the value of man, the search for justice and human advancement for all, the will to participate, the desire for dialogue.

(*Monsignor Charles De Provencheres,*
Letter to the clergy of Créteil, 1968)

Q. *Does the Most Holy Virgin attend your Mass?*
A. Do you think that the Mother does not care for her Son?
Q. *Do the angels attend your Mass?*
A. In a multitude.
Q. *What do they do?*
A. They adore and love.
Q. *Padre, who is closest to your altar?*
A. The entire Paradise.
Q. *Does Our Lord, Padre, love the sacrifice?*
A. Yes, because through it He regenerated the world.
Q. *How much glory does Holy Mass give to God?*
A. Infinite Glory.

God is the scandal. If Christ came back, He would be the scandal; He was at His time and He would be today. My unknown—interpreted by Terence Stamp, made explicit by the presence of his beauty—is not Jesus inserted in a contemporary context, nor is he Eros[11] identified with Jesus; he is the messenger of the unmerciful God, of Jehovah, who by means of a concrete sign, a mysterious presence, removes the mortals from their false security. It is the God who destroys the good conscience, acquired cheaply, under whose shelter live, or rather vegetate, the right-thinkers, the bourgeois, with a false opinion of themselves.

(*Pier Paolo Pasolini,*[12] *in the French periodical* Quinzaine
littéraire, *speaking of his movie* Teorema. *The movie tells*

---

[11] Pagan God of love
[12] Pier Paolo Pasolini was a sordid controversial figure of Italian "intellectual" life. Politically he belonged to the radical Left. He was a homosexual: in his 40s he

*the story of an enigmatic young man who has sexual rela-
tions with all members of the family that hosts him. The
movie was presented at the Venice Film Festival of 1968,
obtaining the prize of the Catholic jury of OCIC*[13])

Q. *What do we have to do during Holy Mass?*
A. To feel pity and love
Q. *Padre, how do we have to attend Holy Mass?*
A. The same way The Most Holy Virgin and pious women did.
The same way St. John attended the Eucharistic sacrifice and the
bloody one of the Cross.
Q. *What benefits do we gain in attending it?*
A. Innumerable ones. You will see them in Paradise.

---

started living with a 15 year old boy, but eventually was killed by a male prostitute
he had picked up in the streets.
[13] OCIC was the International Catholic Organization for Cinema

CHAPTER 3

Not Even One Iota

Padre Pio defends the immutability of the Catholic Mass,
foresees the upcoming revolution, and pleads with the
pope to remove from him the bitter chalice of the liturgical
reform

On Tuesday, March 9, 1965, the monastery of San Giovanni
Rotondo was thrown into turmoil by the arrival of an emissary of
the Roman Curia who needed to talk to Padre Pio. The meeting
took place in an unusual way, because, although the visitor was a
Cardinal of high rank, he preferred to keep the meeting discreet.
In reality, he was delivering an important message and had received
orders not to make the matter public.

For the old Capuchin this was not reassuring in itself, but rather
the opposite. By now, at the end of his earthly life, the poor friar
was just emerging from the latest persecutions, which included
calumnies, maliciousness, threats, revenge, injustices, and deceits
by some close associates of Pope John XXIII in the front line. He
certainly did not need any more trouble at this point. Seeing a
prince of the Holy Roman Church coming especially for him from
Rome might be a good sign, but it might also be the beginning of
new troubles.

Cardinal Antonio Bacci, sent to San Giovanni Rotondo on
behalf of Pope Paul VI, in reality, was carrying good news. Padre
Pio would be allowed to continue celebrating the Mass according
to the rite of all times, the rite of his ordination, the rite that had
forged hundreds of saints, the rite that is conveniently defined
"Tridentine" even though it is filled with centuries of faith and

good doctrine. The pope, who, four years later, would approve the definitive version of the *Novus Ordo Missae* and authorize the inventors of the new rite to impose it with intellectual and pastoral forcefulness of rare efficacy, was allowing the stigmatic friar to steer himself clear from those innovations which had begun to be introduced in the Missal precisely in 1965. Padre Pio had already suffered enough because of the Church and at the hands of too many churchmen: it was not possible to destroy under his very eyes the instrument through which he had offered to the Lord all those pains that agonized him as much as, and perhaps even more than, the stigmata.

Yves Chiron writes in *Padre Pio, a Path of Mercy*: "The authorization to be able to celebrate Mass in Latin until death relieved Padre Pio, who was worried by the various reforms and novelties that were disturbing the Church and rekindling divisions among the fathers at the Council."

In reality, the liturgical reform, which, by perverting the rite, would eventually overturn the altars and the churches, as well as the faith of so many unwary Catholics, was still under development. The reform was being invented *ex novo* by the *Consilium ad exsequendam constitutionem de sacra Liturgia* [Commission for Implementation of the Constitution on the Sacred Liturgy]; the committee appointed for a major role in the editing of the new text of the *Missale Romanum* was headed by Archbishop Annibale Bugnini, strongly suspected of freemasonry. The liturgical reform, in fact, would definitively become fully effective in 1969, but since March 7, 1965, the first Sunday of Lent, some trial experimentations had already taken place. These would, in a short time, irreparably lead to the premeditated revolution. Bugnini's operation was not much appreciated even in the sacred palaces, since, instead of being rewarded with the Cardinal's crimson, he was in haste exiled, in 1976, as Apostolic Nuncio to Iran. But by then it was too late.

The Council? "For pity's sake, finish it off quickly."

Padre Pio understood the results of the reform, or saw its results much in advance. He did not like the spirit of novelty circulating within the Church and was agitated by the sight of the tumultuous ferment shaking the Vatican II Council, by now in its final moments. More than once he had lamented, speaking with sorrow about a "Church without a helmsman," explaining this concept with a juicy comparison: "The fish starts smelling from the head."[1] He said so also to Cardinal Bacci, who asked him, on behalf of the Pontiff, his opinion regarding the Council. "For pity's sake, finish it off quickly."

This episode is revealed in the *Small Chronology for the Cause of Beatification of Padre Pio*, edited by Giuseppe Pagnossin, but it is confirmed by another source, Padre Carmelo of Sessano, a confrere who was for a long time close to the Saint of Pietrelcina. The testimony is reported in an article published in the weekly *Il Settimanale* of January 4, 1975:

> This episode was made public by Padre Carmelo of Sessano, with his blue eyes and the beard of a patriarch, who was first a fellow student of and later, from 1953 to 1958, Father Guardian of Padre Pio. He was outspoken during a press conference which passed almost unknown to the public (in part because of a newspaper strike, in part because of the usual conspiracy of silence) and called for the presentation of the book *Padre Pio of Pietrelcina, the Cyrenean of All*, published by The Franciscan Cultural Center and written by Padre Alessandro of Ripabottoni, of the monastic province of Foggia. […] The meeting, attended by a few reporters and by many very devout people, took place as if in a catacomb in the basement of the Alicorni Hotel, close to St. Peter's, a location selected previously for certain meetings of dissenting priests and of the synodal vanguard. This time though, the protagonist was a priest of the assent and a

---

[1] Italian proverb

traditionalist. Padre Pio, in fact, had always been considered a priest of the old Church, a traditionalist. It was indeed on behalf of the old Church that Padre Pio begged for the closing of the Council. "Our confrere," explained Padre Carmelo of Sessano, "was not so much against the Council, as he was worried about the direction it had taken. He feared the bursting innovations, and he was suspicious of the front from Holland which had already established itself with the Austrians and others." Padre Pio was well aware of the warning against those who intended to change even one iota of the sacred doctrine.

The anti-liturgical heresy

Most of all, Padre Pio had realized that the rising heresy, as it happens in the most difficult times in the life of the Church, was the one which Dom Prosper Gueranger, Benedictine Abbot of Solesmes and great lover of the liturgy, had defined back in the 19th century as "the anti-liturgical heresy." This was an anti-Christ-like movement incessantly on the attack where Christianity was authentic. Dom Gueranger writes in his essay *The Anti-liturgical Heresy and the Protestant Reformation:*

> It has been reserved for Western Christianity to see orga-nized in its bosom the longest war, the most obstinate one that is ongoing still, against the established liturgical acts. Two things contribute to keep the Western Church in such a state of trial: first of all, as I said previously, the vitality of Roman Christianity, the only one deserving the name of Christianity, and by consequence the one against which all the forces of errors must turn. Secondly, the character rationally materialistic of the western populations.

Dom Gueranger, for purely historical reasons, did not see the corrupting action set in motion by modernism and neo-modernism in the 20th century. Nonetheless, he described it ahead of time in the minutest details when he showed the principles and the effects of the Protestant Reformation.

Luther […] did not say anything that his forerunners had not said before him, but he pretended to free man from the subjugation of thought to the teaching power, and, at the same time, from the slavery of the body concerning the liturgical authority.

Not much imagination is necessary to discover that the results of the Lutheran Reformation, exposed by the Abbot of Solesmes in the 1800s, are the same as those which have been scourging the Catholic Church from the 1960s. It suffices to glance at some titles of the paragraphs in Dom Gueranger's work: "Hate for Tradition in the Rubrics of Worship," "Substitution of the Ecclesiastic Formulas with Readings from the Sacred Scriptures," "Insertion of Erroneous Formulas," "Customary Contradiction with the Principles," "Elimination of the Ceremonies and Formulas Expressing the Mysteries," "Extinguishing the Spirit of Prayer," "Elimination of the Intercession of the Blessed Virgin and Saints," "Use of the Vernacular in the Divine Worship," "Reduction of the Number of Prayers," "Hate toward Rome and its Laws," "Destruction of the Priesthood," "The Prince, Head of Religion."

This list of topics, terribly current in the present age, when viewed one century after its draft, resembles indeed the insights of the prophetic gifts of an inspired man. After all, Luther, when talking about the Rome he hated so, explained to his followers: "When we will have turned their altars backwards, we will have destroyed their religion." This is exactly what Padre Pio feared, even more so because the German reformer had carried on his revolution by deceiving men that they could be freed "from the slavery of thought with regard to the teaching power, and from the slavery of the body concerning the liturgical authority." Those two "slaveries" are exactly those upon which the Capuchin of San Giovanni Rotondo had founded his sanctification: the submission to Rome even to the martyrdom of his own thoughts and of his own honor, and the sacrifice at the altar even to the daily martyrdom of his own body and his own soul. The offering of his own was to God to complete the passion of Christ sacrificed on the Cross and, day after day, sacrificed again on the altar. All of this was recapitulated with terrific and sublime efficacy in the Mass that had marked for centuries and centuries the life of peasants and scholars, workers and philosophers, charlatans and pious men, thieves and pilgrims, priest-haters and clericals.

Those Masses are too long

"He used to advance with heavy tread toward the altar at four o'clock in the morning in the presence of a crowd of faithful, poor and rich, so packed as to form one single motionless body, only one mute prayer," the philosopher Jean Guitton recounted in an article published in *La Croix* in 1968.

> He was proceeding with the celebration with increasing suffering, and, when he reached the beginning of the Canon, he stopped as if in front of an impossible climb, a love seen as both painful and radiant, an inexpressible mystery, a mystery capable of making one die. The glance that he was casting upwards, after the Consecration, manifested all of this. I said to myself that perhaps he was the only stigmatic priest in act, while all the others are so virtually.

In reality, since his ordination in August 1910, that Capuchin, after returning home to Pietrelcina because of ill health, already had started to baffle his fellow villagers in the same way he would later baffle the famous philosopher. His Masses were too long, and the people of his village, although they did love him and certainly were not prone to think that he was crazy, could not afford to spend so much time while the work in the fields needed to be done. He might very well be a saint, but it certainly was rather strange that the little friar, who, by continuing to celebrate Masses that lasted hours and hours, ended up in the church all alone. Not even the sacristan could endure it. He used to open the door, make sure that all was in order, and then leave Padre Pio in contemplation of his Jesus.

The rich testimony of Dom Giuseppe Orlando, saved in a typed and still unpublished diary, talks precisely about these times.

Dom Giuseppe was of the same age and village of Padre Pio, but he was not under time pressure for work in the fields as were all the others in Pietrelcina. Nonetheless, he, too, was amazed at that phenomenon. "His Holy Mass was an incomprehensible phenomenon," he narrates.

> I have seen him celebrating Mass on the main altar a few times, but I report what I have been told by Pastor Pannullo, under oath upon his priesthood. Padre Pio, at the point of the *Memento*, was so absorbed in prayer that he would stand still more than one hour without proceeding. His Mass was so long that people avoided it because, as they all had to go to the fields to work, this being a rural village, they could not stay in church for hours and hours to pray with him. The Pastor told me that he had reprimanded him for this; he had even reported him to the Guardian Father of the convent of the Capuchins, who was often coming to Pietrelcina to inquire about the health of his subject. Father Guardian begged the Pastor to call him mentally, so that, by holy obedience, he would obey. Pastor Pannullo, who was not a man who could be taken for a ride, welcomed with skepticism the plea of Guardian Father, and he would have liked to respond in kind, but he pretended to consent. Well, every day that Padre Pio was celebrating Mass, the prelate positioned himself in church and, from a distance, mentally would give orders which Padre Pio promptly obeyed. The Prelate confirmed this to me: "Listen, Peppino, I have one step in the grave and you have to believe that what I said is true."[2]

Like a living host, Padre Pio mystically donated all of himself at the point where the Son of God offered himself to the Father in the supreme sacrifice. "*Hoc est enim Corpus meum...Hic est enim Calix sanguinis mei, novi et aeterni testamenti, mysterium fidei, qui pro vobis et pro multis effundetur in remissionem peccatorum.*" Once again the blood of Jesus was separated from His body and around that sacrifice revolved the whole universe and the eternal life of those who embraced it.

---

[2] "Peppino" is a familiar form of Giuseppe, like "Joey" for Joseph.

"Tell me, why do you suffer so much during Consecration?" his spiritual daughter Cleonice Morcaldi had asked. "Because it is there indeed that a new and admirable destruction and creation happen." The mystery of transubstantiation, the changing in substance of the bread and the wine into the body and the blood of Our Lord Jesus Christ. "In these words," explain the authors of the book *Padre Pio in His Intimacy,*

> Padre Pio encompassed his intimate and mysterious living participation to the tragedy of Golgotha. Here all the mystery of the pain and love of Christ found the highest expression shared by the celebrant Padre Pio, associated to the destruction of his self and his configuration to the Charity of Christ [...]. Up to Communion, in Padre Pio's Mass, you could perceive the progressive flow of what happened on Calvary. Padre Pio, after Consecration, entered into the various moments of the agony of the Crucified up to the "ninth hour"; the seven words of the Jesus in passion, the abandonment, the offering of the Sorrowful Mother to John, up to the *Consummatum est.* That Mass, mystically, was like the one of two thousand years ago and the participants could become, in prayer, part of Calvary.

The world may even survive without the sun, but not without the Holy Mass

The people of Pietrelcina could not be faulted if they did not realize that, in the remote church of St. Ann, a young man of the village was offering himself for their salvation. Neither could one blame that young man who was unable to lend an ear to the call of the earth while his eyes were aiming at Heaven. He was thirsty for the glory of God and the salvation of souls for whom he would have promptly given his life. "If men understood what the Mass is," the Padre used to say, "you would need an army of soldiers to defend the altar from the loving assault of the faithful." And he loved to repeat: "The world may even survive without the sun, but not without the Holy Mass." He used to teach the priests to divide their day in two parts, the first in preparation of the Divine Sacrifice, and the second in thanksgiving.

In one of the diaries kept during the first persecution he suffered at the hands of churchmen, between the end of the 1920s and the beginning of the 1930s, the Friar of Pietrelcina describes what the Mass is all about as Jesus Himself might say. Here is a page published by Francobaldo Chiocci and Luciano Cirri in *Padre Pio, a Victim's Story,* upon which the reformers and their wretched followers should reflect:

> Just think that the priest who calls Me to come into his hands has a power that I did not even concede to my mother; reflect upon the fact that, if, instead of the sacristan, the highest Seraphim were to serve the priest at Mass, they would not be worthy to stay next to him; ask yourselves if, despite the preciousness of the gift I give you, it is still appropriate to be at Mass thinking about anything other than Me. Rather it would be right that you, humbled and thankful, quiver close around Me and offer Me with all your soul to the Father of all mercies; indeed, it would be right to consider the altar, not for what men have made of it, but for its true worth, given My mystic but Real Presence. Look at the Host, in which every species comes to nothing, and there you will see Me humiliated for you; look at the Chalice in which my blood comes back to earth loaded with all sort of benedictions. Offer Me up, offer Me up to the Father, do not forget that it is for this reason that I come back among you.
>
> If they told you: "Let us go to Palestine to get acquainted with the holy places where Jesus lived and died" your heart would jump, would it not? Well, the Altar where I descend now is more than Palestine, because from there I left twenty centuries ago and on the Altar I come back every day alive, true, real, although hidden; but it is I, My very same heart that beats in the hands of My minister, I return to you, not as a symbol, oh no, but for real; I say to you again: for real. [...]
>
> Gethsemane, Calvary, Altar! Three places of which the last one, the Altar, is the sum of the first and second added together;

they are three distinct places, but only in one is He whom you will find there.

[…] I come back, on the holy Altar whence I call you; bring your hearts on the holy corporal that holds my Body, plunge, O beloved souls, into that divine Chalice containing My Blood. There is where love will bind the Creator, the Redeemer, and your Victim to your spirits; there is where you will celebrate My glory in the infinite humiliation of Myself. Come to the Altar, look at Me, think intensely of Me…

The new world needs the old Mass

A few decades of wicked reforms have been sufficient to erase a page so sublime. Deprived of the notion of sacrifice, so many good Catholics burned out, many others lost their faith, and still more have mistaken the faith for charitable works only, lacking doctrine and fervor. The churches have been turned into stages for rallies in the illusion of attracting those far away, ending up, instead, losing the ones who were close. It was believed, according to anti-evangelical logic, that rocking in the world or dancing at the sound of the music of its pipers could bring more fruits than staying still in front of the altar. The thought was that efficiency could bring true salvation in a world that the Church had not yet been able to make perfect. The thought was that the old Mass was too old for a new world.

Quite the opposite: the new world needed that old Mass. To deny that old Mass to the world has been the greatest betrayal ever perpetrated against it. A more dangerous and effective weapon could not have been created for throwing the world into the Enemy's hands. In fact, it is the Mass that holds the world. "The world may exist even without the sun, but not without the Holy Mass." There is no more efficacious shield to hold God's anger before the infidelities of His creatures, of all His creatures. There is no more efficacious instrument to mold those unfaithful creatures into children worthy to enter the Father's house, to forge saints.

Dom Gueranger writes in the golden book, *The Holy Mass*:

There is no doubt that if we were given only the power to adore God, present among us, it still would have been a lot, but now much more has been given to us in Communion. However, the Sacrifice remains well above these first two benefits. Indeed, through the Sacrifice we may act upon God Himself, without Him being entitled to be indifferent to it, because, otherwise He would act against His own glory. And since God has done all things for His own glory, He pays attention to the Sacrifice of the Mass and grants, in one way or another, what has been asked of Him. Thus, not even one Mass is celebrated without accomplishing the four purposes of the great Sacrifice: adoration, thanksgiving, propitiation, petition; and this because God committed Himself to it. When Our Lord, teaching us how to pray, said *Sanctificetur nomen Tuum*, it was already a big request, which concerned greatly the glory of God. Yet in the Holy Mass we have much more: we can tell God that He cannot ignore the Sacrifice, because it is Jesus who offers Himself in it, and that He cannot but hear us, because it is Jesus Christ who prays.

A breach within the walls of the citadel sieged by the Enemy

This Mass Padre Pio had always celebrated and this Mass he wanted to continue to celebrate. The fear that he could no longer do so compelled him to have recourse to the pope, an unusual action for a friar sworn to obedience even to the point of martyrdom. Only the awareness of the gravity of what was taking place and the vision of the horrendous consequences deriving from it must have prompted the old Capuchin to dare so much.

From the very first signs, it was clear that the liturgical reform would obscure the sacrificial aspect of the Mass, enhancing instead the pro-Protestant convivial one. This perturbed the soul of a priest, who, since his ordination wrote:

Jesus, my breath, my life:
Today when trembling
I elevate You

in a mystery of love,
Let me be with You in the world
The way, truth, and life, and for You, a saintly priest,
A perfect Victim.

This was a priest who, in 1916, wrote of himself to his spiritual father: "Thanks to Heaven the victim has already climbed on the altar of the holocausts and by himself, gently, is stretching on it." He wrote to one of his spiritual daughters: "From the altar of the holocausts, my dear daughter, where I am, I will never come down again."

The eclipse of the Mass as a sacrifice would later lead to the eclipse of the Christian Faith, of the Christian way of life, of the Christian light in the world. As we have already mentioned, Dom Gueranger writes: "If the Holy Sacrifice of the Mass should come to an end, it will not take long for us to fall back into the abyss of depravatity where the pagans once were, and this would be the work of the Antichrist." A priest like Padre Pio, "victim[...]ascended on the altar of the holocausts," would never make a gesture, never support an intention aimed at debasing and weakening the efficacy of the divine sacrifice. But this was exactly what was in store, and he, locked in the convent of San Giovanni Rotondo, could see it clearly; he perceived accurately what so many other priests, albeit with impressive titles and in good faith, were unable to foresee.

The Padre understood that the drama of those times, generally considered as the labor pains of the beginning of a new and radiant epoch, was instead unprecedented in the history of the Church. He knew very well that unworthy ministers of God had always been and always would exist. During one of his visions, Jesus manifested to him all His sorrow for the priests who did not correspond to His love: "'Butchers!' And then to me[3] He said: 'My son, do not think that my agony lasted three hours; no, I will be in agony until the end of times, because of the souls I benefited the most.'" But, for as numerous as that crowd who wounded the love of Christ could

---

[3] Padre Pio is speaking here.

be, it consisted nonetheless of individual cases that dishonored the uncorrupted means of the sacrifice. Now instead, the very nature of the means was being betrayed by turning it into something different. It was an open breach within the walls of the citadel under siege by Satan.

A saintly friar in the "age of catastrophe"

The results became evident in the decades that followed. We saw emptied convents and monasteries, decimated vocations, an infatuation for the world and its sweetly anti-Christ sirens, a feverish spirit of continuous reforms with inevitable loss of any sense of hierarchy and obedience, parish priests rebelling against their pastors, pastors revolting against their bishops, bishops dissenting with the pope, sacraments considered a minor bureaucracy to be avoided, deserted confessionals, the practice of prayer annihilated, liturgical creativity to the point of parody, a fading faith in the Real Presence, empty tabernacles and tabernacles removed from the altars, the Blessed Sacrament hidden in the sacristies, altars reduced to workplace cafeteria tables, relics and sacred books sold in flea markets…All of them are bad fruits of the abandonment of the Mass of all time and of the good doctrine which, naturally and supernaturally, goes along with it.

Padre Pio must have seen all of this, since he undertook his unprecedented action of asking the pope for the dispensation from celebrating the new Mass then under preparation. Suffice it to observe that he even accepted to write and sign under dictation declarations relieving his persecutors of any responsibility. He was the one who had suffered silently the most hideous vexations and calumnies from churchmen who were more interested in worldly business and in their own profit than in the salvation of souls. He was also the one who never dared to criticize any of his superiors even when he was treated as a liar, when they denied the evidence of the stigmata given to him by Our Lord.

He, who had suffered all of this treatment in silence, could not concede to celebrate the divine sacrifice according to a Missal invented by some intellectuals according to their own image and likeness. He resisted it in his own style: meekly, but firmly. He was really seeing far into the future, and he knew that he could oppose what he mercilessly called "the age of catastrophe" only by remaining immersed in his Mass, the Mass of the saints. His spiritual daughter Cleonice Morcaldi testifies this in her memoirs, when in grief she narrates her attendance at, after Padre Pio's death, the hasty new Mass of a friar in San Giovanni Rotondo:

> I attended yesterday the Mass celebrated by a friar. My God, what rush! A shocking hurry! It seemed that the carpet was burning under his feet. It happened in the monastery, and he was celebrating on the altar of the Padre. I was told that "they will shorten the Holy Mass even more, and with it the other prayers. The Rosary also is outdated, it is too long, people get tired." The good gets shorter and the bad gets longer. In the movies, in the theaters, in front of the television, people do not get tired; they remain there for hours and hours, day and night. The devil intensifies his work nonstop; God's ministers cut back, shorten everything: Mass, Confession, prayers, worships, homilies, catechisms. "The sons of darkness are more astute than the sons of light!" On this painful decay the Padre did not speak out, he only used to say: "Let us do what we have always been doing, what our fathers have done." I understand now why, years ago, he told me: "I would like never to come down from the altar! I would like to celebrate 60 Masses a day." What I did not understand then, is clear now. He wished to multiply the number of his Masses, to make amends for today's decay. That "tremendous mystery" that made the Padre tremble while approaching the altar of God has been reduced to a hasty reading that stuns you. My God, have pity on your Church! May the Masses of the Padre and those of the good priests make reparation for so much ruin, foreseen and lamented by that pierced heart, who sacrificed himself for You and for your redeemed ones.

Padre Pio, Cardinals Bacci and Ottaviani, and the *Short Critical Study*

"Let us do what we have always been doing, what our fathers have done." Even if not with these exact words, Padre Pio did however entrust his intent, and also his fears, to Cardinal Bacci, who came from Rome to San Giovanni Rotondo to deliver to him the indult granted by the pope for the celebration of the Mass of all times. The peasant friar and the Latin scholar cardinal had the opportunity to reflect on the present times, on the Vatican II drawing to a close: "For pity's sake, finish it off soon."

It is not even a simple coincidence that Cardinal Bacci, together with Cardinal Alfredo Ottaviani, on September 13, 1969, signed the introductory letter for the Holy Father of the *Short Critical Study of the Novus Ordo Missae*. This document, compiled by a qualified group of intellectuals and prelates, highlighted the inconsistencies, the distortions, and, most of all, the grave change of course in Catholic doctrine of the new Missal published in April. This *Critical Study* initiative started within the association Una Voce, and the editing of the text was made, in particular, by Father Guerard des Lauriers and by the writer Cristina Campo. In order to be presented to the Pontiff, it needed authoritative support, and, looking back at those events, we may suppose that this support was found in the two princes of the Church who had dealt personally with Padre Pio: Cardinal Bacci, as he was the evaluator of the traditional point of view of the Capuchin, and who, moreover, as we have seen, acted as a pontifical ambassador; and Cardinal Ottaviani, who was at that time the Prefect of the Congregation for the Doctrine of the Faith, a devotee and protector of Catholic orthodoxy.

Francobaldo Chiocci and Luciano Cirri write:

> Ottaviani, despite the fact that the Holy Office under the direction of his predecessors had a lot to regret regarding the Padre Pio affair, has always been a prudent and convinced admirer of the Capuchin with the stigmata, whom he loved as

a friar of the old Church of suffering, of sacrifice, of rigor. One day Padre Pio confided to a prelate of the Holy Office: "I would not exaggerate if I said that, in my prayers, I remember him and thank him at least 50 times a day." [...] Cardinal Ottaviani assiduously cared also for the health of the Capuchin. One day he personally looked around for a robust friar who would be able to attend concretely to the sick, wounded monk, and even was ready to carry him on his own back if necessary.

We earnestly beseech Your Holiness

Indeed, Providence draws seemingly bizarre plans to the eyes of men. One of those plans links the destinies of Padre Pio and the two princes of the Church in the name of the veneration for the Mass of all times. After an accurate reading of the New Missal just compiled, the *Short Critical Study* presented by Bacci and Ottaviani expressed all the reservations and fears that the Friar of San Giovanni Rotondo, who died the year before its publication, had manifested while it was in the draft stage.

The letter, signed by Cardinals Bacci and Ottaviani, reads as follows:

> Most Holy Father,
> After we and others have examined the *Novus Ordo* Mass prepared by the experts of the "Commission for Implementation of the Constitution on the Sacred Liturgy" [the *Consilium*], and after long deliberation and prayer, we are aware of the duty we have before God and before Your Holiness to express the following considerations:
> 1. The attached brief critical study is the work of a select group of theologians, liturgists, and pastors of souls, and however brief it may be, it examines the novel elements implicit in the *Novus Ordo* Mass, which may be given different interpretations. In doing so, this study demonstrates sufficiently that the *Novus Ordo* Mass represents, overall and in its details, a striking departure from the Catholic theology of the Mass as it was elaborated in Session XXII of the Council of Trent, which, by

permanently fixing the "canons" of the rite, erected an insurmountable barrier against any heresy which could undermine the integrity of the Mystery.

2. The pastoral reasons advanced to justify such a serious rupture do not seem sufficient, even if doctrinal reasons are given to support them. The eternal elements of the Mass, when they are even present, are reduced to a lesser prominence or even moved out of place altogether. So many novelties appear in the *Novus Ordo* Mass that it strengthens and even makes certain the doubt, which unfortunately pervades many circles, that those truths which have always been believed by the Christian people can be changed or ignored without betraying the sacred deposit of doctrine to which the Catholic Faith is bound for eternity. Recent reforms have amply demonstrated that new changes in the liturgy cannot be made without scandalizing the faithful, who are already showing that these changes are unbearable and will undoubtedly diminish their Faith. In consequence, the greater part of the clergy is now undergoing an agonizing crisis of conscience, which we see daily and in countless numbers.

3. We are certain that these considerations which are directly inspired by the vibrant voice of both the pastors and the flock will find their echo in the paternal heart of Your Holiness, who is always so deeply attentive to the spiritual needs of the sons of the Church. Nevertheless, those for whom laws are made have the right and even the duty to ask the legislator to abrogate such laws when they prove to be harmful.

Therefore, at a time when the purity of the Faith and unity of the Church suffer such cruel lacerations and still greater dangers, which every day find an afflicted echo in the words of the common Father, we strongly beseech Your Holiness not to prohibit the possibility of continuing to have recourse to the integral and fruitful Roman Missal of St. Pius V, so highly praised by Your Holiness and so deeply revered and loved by the whole Catholic world.[4]

---

[4] *The Ottaviani Intervention*, Angelus Press. 2015

The oblivion of the sacrifice

At this point it is worth noting the first part of the *Short Critical Study* because it reveals a page of the history of the Church for too long kept hidden.

> In October 1967, the Synod of Bishops was convoked in Rome and was asked for a judgment on the experimental celebration of a so-called "Normative Mass" created by the *Consilium*.
>
> This Mass aroused the most serious misgivings among those present at the Synod, with a strong opposition (43 *non placet*), scores of substantial reservations (62 *juxta modum*), and 4 abstentions, out of 187 voters. The international press spoke of its "refusal" by the Synod, while the more progressive media kept silent. A noteworthy periodical which is directed to bishops and publishes their teaching summed up the new rite as follows: "It intends to wipe out the whole theology of the Mass. Basically it resembles the Protestant theology that has destroyed the sacrifice of the Mass."
>
> In the *Novus Ordo* Mass, promulgated by the Apostolic Constitution *Missale Romanum*, we find substantially that very same "Normative Mass." It does not appear that the Episcopal Conferences as such have even been consulted about it in the meantime. [...]
>
> We begin with the definition of the Mass given at the beginning of the second chapter of the General Instruction of the Roman Missal: "On the Structure of the Mass" (no. 7).
>
> *De structura Missae.*
> *Cena dominica sive Missa est sacra synaxis seu congregatio populi Dei in unum convenientis, sacerdote praeside, ad memoriale Domini celebrandum. Quare de sanctae ecclesiae locali congregatione eminenter valet promissio Christi: "Ubi sunt duo vel tres congregati in nomine meo, ibi sum in medio eorum"* (Mt. 18:20).
>
> On the structure of the Mass.
> The Lord's Supper, or Mass, is the sacred gathering (*synaxis*) of the congregation of the people of God in one assembly, pre-

sided over by a priest, to celebrate the memorial of the Lord. Thus, the Lord's promise—"where two or three are gathered in My name, I am in their midst" (Mt. 18:20)—applies in its highest form to these congregations of the holy local church.

The definition of the Mass is thus limited to that of a "supper," which is continuously repeated (nos. 8, 48, 55, 56).

That "supper" is furthermore characterized by the congregation presided over by the priest, and of the assembly gathered to celebrate the memorial of the Lord by recalling what He did on Holy Thursday.

None of this indicates the Real Presence, nor does it indicate the reality of the Sacrifice, nor the sacramental character of the consecrating priest, nor the intrinsic value of the Eucharistic Sacrifice independent of the congregation's presence.

In a word, this new definition does not contain any of the essential dogmatic principles of the Mass which make up its true definition. The omission of these dogmatic principles in such a definition cannot be involuntary. Purposely omitting these dogmatic principles is equivalent to "surpassing" them, and then to denying them, at least in practice.[5]

Pope Paul VI, perhaps as a consequence of the reading of the *Short Critical Study* or of a speech by Cardinal Charles Journet, made corrections precisely in paragraph 7 of the *Institutio generalis*. However, the Missal was not modified. On this matter Monsignor Nicola Bux writes in his essay, *The Reform of Benedict XVI*:

It is true that Pope Paul VI intended simply to restore the rite of Saint Pius V, that is the liturgy of St. Gregory, but, unfortunately, the experts in the very first stage gained the upper hand by fabricating something altogether different. When the pope realized this, we saw what happened; in the meantime, as the proverb goes, the oxen had run away from the stable. This blunder was precisely the cause of the rift because it revealed that not all had gone the right way.

---

[5] Philosophically, this would be a technical term related to the Hegelian "*aufgehoben*"= "*abrogated*"in the dialectic process.

The problem, as theology and liturgical science showed at that time, and as afterward was proven also by history, was not in one single detail, but in the product as a whole containing all of them. Thus, the sufferings of Padre Pio, in the last and most painful years of his earthly life, were intensified to the point of martyrdom by the awareness of the drama just begun and by the realization that he could not "celebrate 60 Masses a day" to remedy it.

In the religious order with the name of St. Pius X

All of this could not come as a surprise to one of the sons of St. Francis who had chosen upon entering the religious order the name of "Pio" in honor of St. Pius X. Pope Sarto was the pope of the unrelenting fight against the modernist plague, Freemasonry, and Americanism. He was the pope of the good doctrine, of the catechism, of the true and Catholic revival of the liturgy. He was the pope who, in the imminence of the First World War, died after offering in sacrifice to the Lord his own life to prevent the massacre plotted through the hate of what was left of the Christian order in Europe. He was the pope of priestly sanctity. In his Allocution to the bishops on December 12, 1904 he said:

> Who is rich of sanctity—though he may be the least of all—can operate marvelous things for the salvation of the people of God, as proven by many examples in any age and most radiantly in recent memory by John Baptist Vianney, exemplary shepherd of souls. Only sanctity makes the priest as he should be according to his divine vocation: "A man crucified to the world," living in the novelties of a life outstretched toward the things of Heaven to lead the Christian people to them.

This was the portrait of Padre Pio. For his part, the friar tried to conform himself to it as much as possible, certain to find in Pope Sarto a sure guide for his sanctification and for the salvation of souls. On September 7, 1914, three days after the election of the

successor, Benedict XV, the young Capuchin wrote to his spiritual
director:

> Let us wish this newly elected Pontiff to be a genuinely
> worthy successor of that great Pope Pius X. A really noble and
> saintly soul, which Rome had never previously seen the likes of.
> Born of common people, he never was untrue to his humility.
> He really was the supremely good shepherd, the extremely peace-
> ful King, the sweet and meek Jesus on earth. Oh yes! We will
> surely remember the good Pontiff, more to have as an intercessor
> with God Most High, than to lift up to Heaven in our fervent
> prayer for the repose of his great soul. He has been the first, the
> greatest victim of the fratricidal war that deafens with arms and
> armed men and fills with terror all of Europe.

So great was the devotion of the stigmatic friar to Pius X, that
he went in bilocation to visit his tomb inside the Vatican underground, before he was raised to the honor of the altars. Father Luigi
Orione, who was later also canonized, saw him, and reported the
episode to Pope Pius XI. The Pontiff answered in total simplicity:
"If you tell me so, I believe it."

Facing the people or facing the Lord?

What still remains to be clarified at this point is the "liturgical
mystery," found in the images of the last Mass of Padre Pio, that
of September 22, 1968, showing the old friar facing the people.
According to some, this proves that the saint consented to the revo-
lutionary changes imposed by the upcoming reform of the liturgy.
Even more so because, to make the puzzle even more complicated,
Padre Pellegrino, who for a long time was close to the old confrere
narrates:

> In 1966 or 1967 Padre Pio obtained the permission by the
> Holy See to celebrate sitting down and in Latin. The Holy See
> however, imposed two conditions: to celebrate facing the people
> and, only in the doxology of the Eucharistic prayer, to adopt
> the new rite.

In reality, all we have to do is to put the dates in order to discover that Padre Pio cannot be taken for a sponsor of the *Novus
Ordo Missae*. Rather, in this story we can detect another abuse
perpetrated against the saint specifically in what he treasured the
most.

The fact that, after the visit of Cardinal Bacci on March 9,
1965, the Padre continued to celebrate according to the Missal of
all times; this is confirmed by Cleonice Morcaldi in her *Diary*:

> On Christmas night of 1965, the Guardian Father begged
> the Padre to celebrate High Mass. He obeyed. When he got
> to the Creed, while stepping down the steps of the altar to sit
> down, his left foot could not move. The confreres rushed over
> to support him and lead him to the chair. Another day, half way
> during the celebration of the Mass, he turned back to tell the
> altar servers: "I am about to fall!" From that day on he celebrated
> together with a confrere who stood next to him and helped him
> to turn around at the *Dominus Vobiscum*.

It is evident that, up to that time, the Padre did not celebrate
facing the people, but facing the Lord, as he had always done and as
he would have liked to continue doing. It is impossible therefore to
maintain that, in reality, he did not ask to continue to celebrate the
Mass of all times, but that he asked only to celebrate it according
to the Missal of 1965 then still under test, but keeping the Latin
language. It is also difficult to imagine that the friar would go out
of his way to ask for a permission to obtain what the Missal already
offered: the possibility of keeping the Latin. Also, it is not clear why
Pope Paul VI should bother to send to San Giovanni Rotondo a
cardinal to allow a priest, as an extraordinary measure, something
his confreres were already permitted as an ordinary option and
still is today. So, if logic still has some bearing, we must come to
the conclusion that Padre Pio's request was quite different: namely,
that it could only be the petition for the permission to continue
to celebrate according to the Missal prior to the reform, as revised
by John XXIII in 1962. This explains the request to consider the

Mass celebrated by the Padre at four o'clock in the morning as a *Missa sine populo,* "without people," independent of the presence of an assembly. It also explains the existence of pictures showing him in the years 1966 to 1967 celebrating sitting down and facing the Lord and not the people.

The last station of the Way of the Cross

The testimony of Padre Pellegrino is said to have been given between 1966 and 1967, a time period not very accurately stated, but it is confirmed in the *Diary* of Morcaldi:

> The Guardian asked permission from the superiors and the Padre celebrated sitting down, facing the people. How much did we suffer! We believed, we hoped that this was a short term solution; instead, we never saw again the dear Padre celebrating standing up. Pains over pains, torments over torments, and helplessness over helplessness accrued. It was all a painful Way of the Cross! I told him in Confession: "My Padre, I am tired of seeing you suffer and suffering myself. Tell me at least if this is the last station of your Way of the Cross." Sighing he said: "Yes, it is the last one, but remember that it is the longest, the most painful and excruciating one." He paused then he continued: "I am agonizing. It is all about leaving my life!"

After the one of 1965, there was then another request regarding the celebration of the Mass, this time due to the health conditions of the Padre. It was surely after the Christmas festivities, and the time was 1966, as indicated also by Padre Pellegrino. What is most surprising and hurtful in this affair is the fact that the permission to celebrate sitting down was combined with the imposition to face the people and to use the final doxology of the Eucharistic prayer according to the ongoing changes in the Missal.

It really was the last station of the *Way of the Cross*, "the longest, the most painful and excruciating one." Upon a man who, as he himself said, was agonizing in the expectation of "leaving his life," was the overbearing pressure to turn him away from his Mass. At least Providence willed that the Padre was not subjected to the revolution enacted in 1969. In any case, the holy meekness of that friar, who became a living host, surely would have been always stronger than any profane violence.

In light of all this, the images of the last Mass become even more heartrending, the moment in which the last violence was perpetrated against a suffering Padre Pio, already in agony, forced to obey a Guardian Father looking for honor and glory. That was not his Mass. His Mass was the one at four 'o clock in the morning, that Mass the pope had allowed him to continue to celebrate as he had always done, the Mass of his ordination. On that September 22, 1968, he was facing the people, this is true. But, was he seeing them? His eyes, already unable to look down on the earth, just like his soul, were looking up to Heaven where his Lord was awaiting him. The victim had laid himself on the altar of the holocausts, as he himself had said many years earlier. Shortly after that, all would be accomplished.

CHAPTER 4

The Missal Recovered

Padre Pio remains faithful to the Mass of St. Francis, and, as his spiritual son, he discovers that the future of the Church is in its Tradition

A little more than 40 years have passed since Padre Pio's death, but the saint of the stigmata would struggle quite a bit today to recognize the majority of his confreres.

Different times. Or different Capuchins? In any case, mixing in the right proportions the two hypotheses, we arrive at worrisome signs of the times. For instance, a random and objective browse through the internet site of the Italian Capuchins reveals, among similar statements, the following *Franciscans' appeal for peace* signed by the provincial ministers of the Franciscan families of Italy, of which, precisely, Padre Pio's confreres are members:

> We, provincial ministers of the Italian Franciscan families gathered together in Loreto for the annual assembly, in this historical moment, both delicate and poignant of consequences, strongly feel the urgency and the responsibility to announce, despite all, peace.
>
> War is not inevitable; peace is always possible, if we want it. As sons of St. Francis, unarmed prophet and prophet for all, we announce to you: "Peace." Peace is not only an objective to achieve at any cost, but is the principle and foundation of an alternative way to be together on this planet. Peace is built with peace, not with war. Peace is built with justice and freedom, with solidarity and commitment of all for all, without distinction. Uniting our voice to that of the poor in this world, to you, the powerful on this earth, we announce peace. In communion

with the Holy Father John Paul II and with all the peacemakers, we ask God for the gift of peace. With our hearts turned toward Assisi we hope to see the colors of the rainbow rise upon the lands devastated by violence and death. We ask God, father of the whole human family, to give us a heart at peace, capable of overcoming divisions and prejudices; cultural, religious and racial barriers; selfish interests and blind nationalisms, a heart capable of hoping beyond every hope, capable of sharing the expectations and dreams of men and women of our time, a heart capable of bending down with love on the wounds of humanity and to pour upon all the freshness of a new life and the certainty of a better tomorrow.

Dated March 13, 2003, this document is congruent with many other writings preceding and following it on the internet sites, in the magazines, in the preaching, in the catechesis, in the apostolate, and in the pastoral work of the religious order: Through 30 lines, under a deep vacuum of patched-up *ecclesialese*, which is progressive and theologically correct, it seems that the main concern of the sons of St. Francis is to hide Jesus Christ. Such a concern even makes sense, because we could not understand how Our Lord should have to deal with some sort of Peace with the capital "P," raised to the rank of a new divinity of a Pantheon worthy of the psychedelic fantasies of the hippies gathered in convention at Woodstock.

The bitter fruits of sister creativity

We must be realistic and, even if it is painful, we should not be surprised if the panorama presented by the majority of the Capuchins today is the one just described. The only strictness left in an order that was once glorious is limited to the application of all the cornerstones of the boring and very predictable contemporary theology, just as it happens in broad sectors of the contemporary ecclesial world. For the rest, there is some sort of "free for all" with respect to doctrine, mystical practice, and discipline. The sons of Saint Francis of the third millennium themselves explain this on their website:

In our times the way of living of the Capuchins in Italy, in Europe, and in many other countries, mirrors in substance a multi-secular style of Franciscan life, simple and austere, close to the people, developed day after day in brotherhood and prayer. Such description, of course, applies to the majority of friars, keeping in mind that some "creative minorities," attracted by opposite polarities, follow ways of living ranging from pauperism to conformity to the world pushed to the extreme.

The fusion that happens, year after year, between the individual and the fraternity is made easier by a structural weakness in the guidance from the hierarchy, which may be renewed every three years. In a climate of spontaneity, familiarity, and immediacy, one can strengthen a "brotherly personality," open, flexible, steady in listening, unstable in regard to structures, sensitive and disenchanted and, because of this, sympathetic and in syntony with the simple and poor people.

In such a vital frame, every community is "a world in itself," very variable, as spiritual and socio-ecclesial "individual personalities" make their appearance. To open the door of a monastery or a fraternity of Capuchins means to always renew the surprise of a new encounter, unpredictable, in any case, and on the whole enjoyable.

Given these premises, how can one doubt the "surprise of a new encounter, unpredictable" awaiting the naive visitor beyond "the door of a monastery or fraternity of Capuchins"? This is the least that can happen where there is in force a "structural weakness in the guidance from the hierarchy," at the mercy of "creative minorities" with the aim of producing a "brotherly personality open, flexible, steady in listening, unstable in regard to structures, sensitive and disenchanted and, because of this, sympathetic and in syntony with the simple and poor people."

"Throw them out! Throw them out!"

Now that the Capuchins of the third millennium have made their self-introduction, it is easier to understand how right Padre

Pio was when he feared the changes to the *Constitutions* of the
Order, readily begun right after the Vatican II Council.

In 1966, the Father General of the Order arrived in San
Giovanni Rotondo from Rome to ask for the benediction of the
saint in protection of the slippery enterprise.

> Padre, I came to recommend to you the special chapter for
> the new *Constitutions*, said the Father General, coming across
> him in the corridor. Well, as soon as the Padre heard the men-
> tion of new *Constitutions*, he had a violent reaction: "It is all a
> bunch of babble and disasters." Embarrassed, the Superior tried
> to justify himself by explaining the needs of the new generations.
> The saint blasted him: "The head and the heart are missing.
> These two things are lacking, brain and love." Then he walked
> slowly to his cell and, when he reached the door, turned around
> and pointing his finger said: "Let us not pervert ourselves. On
> the day of God's judgment, St. Francis will not recognize us as
> his sons."

We definitely must take the warning seriously, because, always
according to the self-certification on their website, we discover that

> ...in Italy the activity of the Capuchins favors initiatives and
> social activities to help the poor, with great sensitivity for the
> new various needs for social service that surface in the various
> districts of the provinces. Moreover, from the ecclesial stand-
> point, the Capuchins dedicate much energy to the sacrament
> of Reconciliation, according to the examples of St. Leopold
> Mandic and of San Pio of Pietrelcina. Finally, even if in a para-
> doxical way, we should not forget the "apostolic" action of the
> friars who pray and offer their sufferings and their old age for
> the reign of God.

Just so, then, a life like Padre Pio's, consumed in suffering,
offered in sacrifice for the salvation of souls, would be "apostolic"
only within quotes and even a little "paradoxical," using the word
of the Capuchins.

How could the saint be in the wrong if, in 1967, he had an outburst even against the Assistant General[1] of the Order, who ventured to exalt the changes in the *Constitutions*: "What are you doing there in Rome? What are you up to? These people want to touch up even the Rule of St. Francis."

"Padre, we make these changes because the young people do not want to hear about tonsure, habit, bare feet..."

"Throw them out! Throw them out! Tell me ... is it they who do St. Francis the favor of wearing the habit and following his way of life, or is it St. Francis who gives them a gift?"

Woe to him who will betray St. Francis

The Saint of Pietrelcina could not quite tolerate that the Founding Father should be betrayed. He, who like Francis, was bearing in his flesh the same wounds of Jesus crucified; who, like Francis, had become the image of Christ in the suffering offered in sacrifice to the Father; and who, like Francis, had stripped himself of any proud self-love, could not see an error more densely packed with tragic consequences than that of betraying the teachings of the Saint of Assisi.

Those young people who did not want to hear about the habit, the tonsure, the bare feet, in their naïve and presumptuous objective to keep pace with the times and embrace the world, in reality were turning their back to Christ. In exactly the same manner they were getting ready to turn the altars in order to celebrate liturgies more appealing to the taste of a world which was set openly against Christ.

Padre Pio knew this all too well: "Throw them out! Throw them out!" He had said this about these friars. He had lashed out against them with a harshness that too many Catholics, convinced that they must be the sugar, not the salt of the earth, cannot understand. But the Padre knew too well that it is possible to follow St.

---

[1] Definitóre (generale)—A religious who assists his superior in the government of a religious order:

Francis only along the way of the Cross. And likewise, he knew too
well that the refusal of the habit, of the tonsure, of the bare feet were
the start, if not even the end, of an entirely different kind of path.

Many years earlier, in 1915, he had written to his spiritual
daughter Anita Rodote, Franciscan Tertiary:

> Yes, Anita, may your way of living be all heavenly; that is
> our duty as Christians and also as sons of the seraphic father
> St. Francis. As imitators of our seraphic father let us love, more
> than anybody else, Jesus in His passion; let us meditate often the
> pains of the God-Man, and it will not be long before the great
> desire to suffer more and more for the love of Jesus will ignite
> in us. The love for the Cross has always been a distinctive mark
> of chosen souls; to be burdened with the Cross has always been
> a special predilection from the heavenly Father for such souls.
> Our seraphic father well understood that without love for the
> Cross not much profit can be derived on the ways of Christian
> perfection; therefore he always carried engraved in his soul the
> passion and death, as well as all the mortal life of the Son of God
> made man. Fruit of such a tireless meditation was the kindling
> in his heart of an unlimited love for suffering, so that often, rapt
> in an ecstasy of love, he used to exclaim: "So great is the good
> I expect that any pain is a delight." Anita, let us show ourselves
> as worthy children of such a great father. Jesus invites us, too, to
> ascend with Him the way to Calvary. So, let us not refuse to do
> it. To climb the sorrowful mount with Jesus will turn out to be
> sweet for us. We also will not lack mortifications in the course
> of our life: let us love them, let us embrace them with a merry
> soul and let us bless always and in everything the good God.

Luminous meditations versus
nocturnal conversations

One can almost see the shaking heads of those Capuchins,
who could not, and cannot, bear even the weight of the habit or
the discomfort of bare feet. It is hard to imagine that their ways
could cross the *via dolorosa* of Padre Pio. Poor preys of the world's

temptations, which are designed to eradicate from the heart of man the need for sacrifice and, by consequence, to make the Cross of Christ incomprehensible.

In his book *Nocturnal Conversations in Jerusalem*, Cardinal Carlo Maria Martini, one of the most influential exponents of such a theological deviation, explains that he had "had some difficulties with God." Like so many other Christians at the mercy of the world, the illustrious purple-wearing religious could not understand why Our Lord would have allowed His Son to suffer on the Cross: "Even as a Bishop, sometimes I could not look at a Crucifix because the question was tormenting me."

The Capuchins oblivious to St. Francis certainly are more sons of the Jesuit Archbishop of Milan than of their Confrere of San Giovanni Rotondo, being both architects and, at the same time, products of a radical inversion of the concept of man and his relationship with God. This is no longer the result of a fundamentally religious understanding of human nature, but of a strictly intellectual and rationalistic analysis. It is clear that the two viewpoints are in contrast with each other and that the one cannot subsist if the other is present, under penalty of a patent schizophrenia. It is even clearer that, when facing the need for happiness which lies deep in the heart of all men, only one perspective can answer coherently with the Cross, which appears to the other as an inexplicable folly. The one answers with the virtue of religion, the other with the pride of intelligence.

"People who do not think distress me," continues Cardinal Martini. "I would like to have individuals who think. This is the main point. Only then can we ask if they are believers or non-believers." Padre Pio, of the school of St. Francis, would have said exactly the opposite: "People who do not believe distress me. I would like to have individuals who believe. This is the main point. Only then can we ask if they are thinkers or non-thinkers."

The heavenly repetitions of the rosary

Padre Pio could afford clairvoyance like this, such a capability to see things clearly, because he was taken by the love for the holy repetition of the rosary. He was absorbed in the delicate and smooth flow of the beads of the *Ave Maria*, *Pater*, and *Gloria*, of this celestial rhyme so suavely repetitive to make palpable the stillness of time and the incorruptibility of Heaven. However, to relish even the most earthly benefits from it one must become like a child, just like that friar, who, during his whole life, never articulated a homily, never held a lecture, never interpreted according to his own whim any verse of Scripture, never dared to produce any original thought about the Church and its doctrine. And precisely because of this, because of his renunciation of intellectual pride, he had been rewarded with true wisdom, with that specific disposition of the heart that leads one never to become tired of what continues to be repeated in tireless and angelical rhymes.

Indeed, you have to be in the fullness and depth of this infancy so that in your spiritual existence you savor the most amazing side of what you keep on repeating. Vice versa, there is no crueler trap for the adult intelligence in today's world. This is explained in *Orthodoxy* by G. K. Chesterton:

> The modern world as I found it was solidly based on modern Calvinism, on the necessity that things had to be the way they were. But as soon as I started asking questions, I realized that there was no proof for these inevitable repetitions of things, besides the fact that they kept on repeating themselves. Now, as far as I am concerned, the pure repetition made me see things as if generated by something magic rather than by a rational principle.

All the materialistic views of the world, including those from exponents who call themselves Christians, are based on the false principle that repetitive things are dead like the mechanism of a clock. They theorize that if the universe were a living thing, it would show variety. Yet, it would not take much to understand that the change in human things is caused in general by a break to the force that sustains them and, above all, by death.

The idea that variety is linked to life is absurd; instead the inexhaustible, absolute, immortal divine freedom is the ultimate warranty of the repetitiveness of things. Only a God who is unpredictably generous and good beyond any limit can tell the sun every morning to rise again. Chesterton goes on:

> It may not necessarily be an automatic necessity the one that makes little roses all look alike. Maybe God makes them separately, one by one, and He never gets bored making them. Perhaps He has the eternal longing of infancy; because we have sinned and we aged, but Our Father is younger than us. Repetitions in nature may not be simply something that happens over and over, but they may be encores, like onstage.

Hands, feet, and side were dripping blood

The 40 and even 50 rosaries that Padre Pio lifted up every day to Heaven were made with those little roses that the Creator takes the trouble to make one by one so that men may enjoy them and so that they elevate just as many praises to His glory.

The authors[2] of the book *Padre Pio in His Inner Being* write:

> There is no doubt that if Padre Pio lived with the stigmata, he also lived with the rosary beads. Both these mysterious and indissoluble elements are manifestations of his interior world. They materialize his condition of being crucified with Christ and "one" with Mary.[...] Visions, apparitions and ecstasies of his infancy were works of the celestial Mother to make him pure and spotless so as to enable Her to project into his soul that *fiat* of the day of the Annunciation which allowed the Holy Spirit to conceive Jesus in him.

---

[2] Fathers Attilio Negrisolo, Nello Castello, and Stefano M. Manelli

With the rosary in his hands, that Friar of Pietrelcina was getting ready to receive on his body the same signs that united the Saint of Assisi to the passion of Christ.

On the morning of September 20, 1918, shortly after dawn, Fra[3] Pio was alone in the church of the convent of San Giovanni Rotondo. The Father Superior had gone to San Marco in Lamis for the feast of St. Matthew, and the beggar friar was around town with his shoulder bags to do his duty. The Friar of Pietrelcina was immersed in prayer in the choir after a very long Mass where he had recommended to God the many deceased souls of the victims of the Spanish flu epidemic. It was then that a "Person" with "hands, feet, and side dripping blood" appeared to him. This is how he himself describes the event in a letter to his spiritual director on October 22:

> I yielded to a drowsiness similar to a sweet sleep. All the internal and external senses and even the very faculties of my soul were immersed in indescribable stillness. In all this, absolute silence surrounded me. I was suddenly filled with great peace and abandonment which effaced everything else, and all this happened in a flash. While this was taking place I saw before me a mysterious Person similar to the one I had seen on the evening of August 5. The only difference was that his hands and feet and side were dripping blood. His sight terrifies. What I felt in that moment is indescribable. I felt I was dying and really I should have died if the Lord had not intervened and strengthened my heart, which was about to burst out of my chest. The vision of the Figure disappeared and I became aware that my hands, feet and side were dripping blood! Imagine the anguish I experienced then and continue to experience almost every day; the wound in my heart bleeds continually, especially from Thursday evening until Saturday.[4]

---

[3] "Fra" literally means "brother": the authors here, and later in the text, prefer to stress the humility of Padre Pio, especially so early in his life, by referring to him as a "brother," although he was already an ordained priest.

[4] Padre Pio of Pietrelcina, *Letters* (Our Lady of Grace Capuchin Friary, Italy, 1984), Vol. 1, pp. 1217-1218.

A sublime gift

Sweetness and suffering, joy and fright, reverence and fear: the same as St. Francis in La Verna on September 17, 1224. The Seraphic Father, too, received the stigmata of Jesus while in prayer in view of the feast of St. Michael the Archangel, in whose honor, says St. Bonaventure in his *Legenda Minor*, Francis was dedicating a penance. St. Bonaventure writes:

> Francis, faithful servant and minister of God, two years before giving up his spirit to God, withdrew into a high and solitary place, called Mount Verna, to make a penance of 40 days in honor of St. Michael the Archangel. From the start, he felt more abundantly than usual the sweetness of the contemplation of divine things and, inflamed even more by celestial desires, he felt himself favored more and more with inspirations from above. One morning, when the feast of the Exaltation of the Holy Cross was near, collected in prayer at the top of the mountain, while he was transported to God by seraphic ardors, he saw the figure of a Seraphim descending from Heaven. He had six wings shining and flaming. With a swift flight he arrived and stopped, raised from earth, next to the man of God. At that point he appeared not only winged, but also crucified.
>
> At this sight Francis was filled with wonder and in his soul there were, at the same time, sorrow and joy. He felt an overwhelming joy seeing Christ in a benevolent aspect, appearing to him in a way as much admirable as affectionate, but, seeing Him nailed like that on the Cross, his soul got wounded by a sword of empathetic sorrow.
>
> After an arcane and intimate conversation, when the vision disappeared, it left in his soul a seraphic fervor and, at the same time, left in his flesh the external signs of the Passion, as if seals had been impressed on his body, made tender by the melting strength of fire.
>
> Soon marks of the nails began to appear on his hands and feet; on the hollow part of his hands and on the upper part of his feet appeared the nail heads, on the other side the tips of the

nails. The right side of the body, as if pierced by a spear, was cut through by a red wound, that bled often.

It was such a sublime gift from Heaven that Pope Benedict XI, since 1304, willed that the remembrance of it be celebrated every year on September 17, and Pope Paul V, to light up in the hearts of the faithful the love for Jesus crucified, in 1615, extended the celebration to the whole Church. So the Missal was enriched with a new feast and with the proper prayers for that day.

Those holy tears

In the Mass that Padre Pio always wanted to celebrate, and for which he refused to follow the imprudence and arrogance of the reform implemented after the Vatican II Council, the *Collect* of September 17, Feast of the Stigmata of St. Francis, reads:

> *Domine Jesu Christe, qui frigescente mundo, ad inflamman-dum corda nostra tui amoris igne, in carne beatissimi Francisci passionis tuae sacra stigmata renovasti: concede propitius; ut ejus meritis et precibus crucem jugiter feramus et dignos fructus poeni-tentiae faciamus.*

> O Lord Jesus Christ, Who, when the world was growing cold, in order to enkindle in our hearts the fire of Thy love, didst renew the sacred marks of Thy Passion on the body of blessed Francis: mercifully grant, that with the aid of his merits and prayers we may ever bear our Cross, and bring forth worthy fruits of penance.

And in the *Postcommunion:*

> *Deus, qui mira crucis mysteria in beato Francisco Confessore tuo multiformiter demonstrasti: da nobis, quaesumus, devotionis suae semper exempla sectari, et assidua ejusdem crucis meditatione muniri.*

> O God, Who in diverse ways didst show forth in blessed Francis, Thy Confessor, the wondrous mysteries of Thy Cross,

grant we beseech Thee, that ever following the example of his devotion, we may be strengthened by constant meditation on that Cross.

It is legitimate, even obligatory and an action yielding good spiritual fruits to ask ourselves how the heart of Padre Pio was disposed when he ascended to the altar that day. However, to answer such a question would be futile and not at all fitting given the level at which eternity descends to soothe the painful transience of created beings. The veil that makes the gift of grace lovingly mysterious cannot be torn. We must limit ourselves to contemplating the tears of the crucified God coming to mingle with the ones of men. Padre Pio, like Brother Francis, had the gift of tears, melted veils of the most pure modesty that envelop what is unutterable, sheltering it from profane looks. They are the smallest vessels, those short-lived products of human flesh, within which the immensely great manifests itself: all that is allowed to the mystic vision in this world.

Jesus, as He did also at Lazarus's tomb, cries because of man and at every time the true miracle happens: instead of Heaven wetting the earth with its rain, the earth wets Heaven with its tears.

On the body of the Seraphic Father and of his spiritual son of San Giovanni Rotondo, this prodigy materializes in silvery threads purified in the painful joy of the signs of Christ's passion. They are tears from the soul, mirror of a delicate harmony between the heaviness of the world and the lightness of grace, a phenomenon almost impossible to represent. Jean-Loup Charvet, in his essay *The Eloquence of Tears*, writes:

> The instant of real tears is the one when the lightness of light and the weight of shadow meet. The two forces do not keep each other under restraint, but in equilibrium. For the true tear, heaviness and darkness are but a memory, but a memory needed for its lightness, indispensable to its light.

Padre Gemelli: science *versus* mystery

If Padre Agostino Gemelli, Franciscan, doctor, and psychologist, had lent an ear to the benevolence of mystery rather than to the ruthlessness of science, he would have judged differently the stigmata of Padre Pio.

Sent by the Secretary of the Holy Office, he arrived in San Giovanni Rotondo in 1920, but he could not examine the wounds of the friar, as the Padre refused to have them observed without a written request. The visitor did not take it kindly, and, even though he had not examined the stigmata, expressed a negative and irrevocable judgment: "Padre Pio has all the somatic characteristics of a hysteric and psychopath.[...] Therefore, the wounds he shows on his body[...] are counterfeit,[...] fruit of a pathological obsessive action."

Such a judgment, based without clinical examination, would nonetheless affect the life of the stigmatic friar because of the prestige of the source. As a result of this event, on May 31, 1923, the Holy Office released a decree declaring that *non constat de supernaturalitate* [there is nothing supernatural] in the facts examined. The formulation did not exclude the possibility of a change of opinion, but, in the meantime, it started the first persecution against the Friar of Pietrelcina. The investigation ended with the fifth decree of condemnation, dated May 23, 1931, in which the faithful were invited not to consider as supernatural the psychiatric manifestations as certified by Padre Gemelli. The first stigmatic priest in history was forbidden to celebrate Mass in public and to hear confessions.

The will of God hidden in the Missal

A son of St. Francis, marked as the Saint of Assisi was by the wounds of the passion of Christ, was forbidden to do in public what St. Francis, who was not a priest, held as most precious: the divine sacrifice, the transubstantiation of bread and wine into the body, blood, soul, and divinity of Our Lord.

Indeed, it was exactly the Mass that the saint of Assisi loved
most of all, even though nowadays he is passed off as the prophet
of tragicomic deviations ranging from pacifism to separate collection of recyclable rubbish, and continuing through egalitarianism
and a misunderstood ecumenism. They would like to present him
almost like a Luther *ante litteram* [forerunner of Luther], possessed
by the hermeneutic of the Word and in rebellion against Rome.
However, Francis had looked for inspiration to found a new religious order precisely from within the Roman Missal. Nothing
more Catholic than this, and, therefore, well removed from the
Protestant heresy, as the *Fioretti*[5] tell us:

> Now, when Messer Bernard had seen by the light of the lamp
> the very devout actions of St. Francis, and had reverently con-
> sidered the words which he spake, he was touched and inspired
> by the Holy Ghost to change his life. Wherefore, when day was
> come, he called St. Francis and said unto him: "Friar Francis, I
> am altogether disposed in my heart to renounce the world and
> to follow thee in that which thou shalt command me." Hearing
> this, St. Francis rejoiced in spirit and said: "Messer Bernard,
> this which you speak of is so great and difficult a work, that we
> ought to seek the counsel of Our Lord Jesus Christ touching
> the same, and to pray Him to vouchsafe to show us His will
> therein and teach us how we may bring the same to good effect.
> Wherefore let us go together to the house of the bishop, where
> there is a good priest, and him will we cause to say Mass, and
> afterward we will continue in prayer until terce, beseeching
> God that, in three openings of the missal, He may show us the
> way which it is His will that we should choose." Thereto Messer
> Bernard made answer that he was well content. Wherefore they
> presently departed and got them to the Bishop's house; and after
> they had heard Mass and had continued in prayer until terce,
> the priest, at the request of St. Francis, took the missal, and
> having made the sign of the most holy cross, opened it three
> times in the name of Our Lord Jesus Christ. At the first open-

---

[5] *The Little Flowers of St. Francis*, tr. W. Heywood, (Methan and Company, 1906),
Chapter 2.

ing, they found that saying which Christ spake in the Gospel to the young man which inquired the way of perfection: "If thou wilt be perfect, go and sell that thou hast, and give to the poor and follow me." At the second opening, they found that saying which Christ spake to the apostles, when He sent them forth to preach: "Take nothing for your journey, neither staff, nor scrip, nor shoes, nor money"; intending thereby to teach them that they ought to set all their hope of living upon God, and to turn all their thoughts to preaching the Holy Gospel. At the third opening of the missal they found that saying which Christ spake: "If any man will come after me, let him deny himself and take up his cross and follow me." Then said St. Francis to Messer Bernard: "Behold the counsel which Christ gives us. Go then, and do thoroughly that which thou hast heard, and blessed be Our Lord Jesus Christ who hath vouchsafed to show us His evangelic way." When he had heard this, Messer Bernard departed and sold all that he had; and he was very rich. And with great rejoicing he gave everything to widows, to orphans, to prisoners, to monasteries, to hospitals, and to pilgrims; and in everything St. Francis faithfully and providently aided him.

Let all mankind tremble when Christ makes Himself present

The writings of St. Francis are star-spangled with acts of love for the Mass and for the Most Holy Sacrament. His testament says:

Of the Most High Son of God Himself I can see in this world nothing else bodily, but His Most Holy Body and His Most Holy Blood. [...] I want that these very holy mysteries above all things be honored, venerated, and placed in precious places.

In the *First Letters to the Custodians*,[6] the saint of Assisi writes:

---

[6] This and the following citations from the letters of St. Francis are, with minor changes, adapted from *The Writings of St. Francis of Assisi*, tr. Paschal Robinson (Dolphin Press, Philadelphia, 1905).

I entreat you more than if it were a question of myself that, when it is becoming and it may seem to be expedient, you humbly beseech the clerics to venerate above all the most holy Body and Blood of Our Lord Jesus Christ and the holy names and words written of Him which consecrate the body. The chalices, corporals, ornaments of the altar, and all that pertain to the Sacrifice ought to be precious. And if they were to find the most holy Body of the Lord lodged very poorly in any place, let It according to the command of the Church be placed by them and kept in a precious place, and let It be carried with great veneration and administered to others with discretion. Also the writings containing the names and words of the Lord, wheresoever they may be found in unsuitable places, let them be collected, and be put in a proper place. And in all the preaching you do, admonish the people concerning penance and that no one can be saved except he that receives the most sacred Body and Blood of the Lord, and that while It is being sacrificed by the priest on the altar and It is being carried to any place, let all the people on bended knees render praise, honor, and glory to the Lord God living and true.

In his *Letter to the Whole Religious Order*, mainly dedicated to the Mass, in the paragraph "On the reverence toward the Body of the Lord" we read:

Wherefore, brothers, kissing your feet and with all the charity of which I am capable, I conjure you all to show all reverence and all honor possible to the most holy Body and Blood of Our Lord Jesus Christ, in Whom the things that are in Heaven and the things that are on earth are pacified and reconciled to Almighty God.

This *Letter* goes on next with the sublime passage entitled "About Holy Mass," a page that needs to be read in its entirety, were it not only for the delight derived from it by every soul even marginally reverent toward the beauty of celestial things and imprinted by the fear of God:

I also beseech in the Lord all my brothers who are and shall be and desire to be priests of the Most High that, when they wish to celebrate Mass, being pure, they offer the true sacrifice of the Body and Blood of Our Lord Jesus Christ in purity, with reverence, with a holy and clean intention, not for any earthly motive or fear or for the love of any man, as if they were to please men. But let every will, in so far as the grace of the Almighty helps, be directed to Him, desiring thence to please with the Mass the High Lord Himself alone because He alone works there in it as it may please Him. For He Himself says: "Do this for a commemoration of me": if any one doth otherwise, he becomes the traitor Judas and is made guilty of the Body and Blood of the Lord. Call to mind, priests, my brothers, what is written of the Law of Moses: how those transgressing it even only materially died by the decree of the Lord without any mercy. How much more and worse punishments he deserves to suffer who hath trodden under foot the Son of God and hath rendered the Blood of the testament unclean by which he was sanctified and hath offered an affront to the Spirit of grace. For man despises, soils, and treads under foot the Lamb of God when, as the Apostle says, not discerning in his judgment or not distinguishing the holy bread of Christ from other nourishments or works, he either eats it unworthily or, if he be worthy, he eats it in vain and unbecomingly, although the Lord has said by the prophet: "Cursed be the man that doth the work of the Lord deceitfully." And the Lord condemns the priests who will not take this to heart sincerely saying: "I will curse your blessings."

Hear ye, my brothers: If the Blessed Virgin Mary is so honored, as is meet, because she bore Him in her most holy womb; if the blessed Baptist trembled in joy and did not dare to touch the holy forehead of God; if the sepulchre in which He lay for some time is venerated; how holy, just, and worthy ought he to be who touches with his hands, who receives with his heart and his mouth, and proffers to be received by others Him who is now no more to die but to triumph in a glorified eternity: on whom the angels desire to turn their gaze! Consider your dignity, brother priests, and be holy because He Himself is holy. And as the Lord God has honored you above all men through this mystery, even so do you also love and reverence and honor Him above all men. It would be a great misery and a deplorable wretchedness when you have Him thus present, to care for anything else in the whole world. Let the entire humanity be seized with fear; let the whole universe tremble; let heaven exult when Christ, the Son of the Living God, makes Himself present on the altar in the hands of the priest. O admirable height and stupendous condescension! O sublime humility! O humble sublimity that the Lord of the universe, God and the Son of God, so humbles Himself that for our salvation He hides Himself under the appearance of a morsel of bread! Consider, brothers, the humility of God and pour out your hearts before Him; and be ye humbled that ye may be exalted by Him. Do not therefore keep back anything for yourselves that He may receive you entirely who gives Himself up entirely to you.

The Franciscans and the Tridentine Missal

This is the fount where Padre Pio was quenching his thirst, with body and soul burning of the same thirst for God that had scorched the soul and body of St. Francis. His gaze, fixed towards Heaven, could not contemplate any other sacrifice, could not live on any other sight than the one of the Crucifix, could not delight in any other Mass. Proof of this was his disclosure to Cleonice Morcaldi when his spiritual daughter asked him in whose arms he would be laid down after his mystic death in the divine sacrifice: "In the arms of St. Francis."

Even more so because the Capuchin of Pietrelcina, in the bosom of the Franciscan family, was in the cradle of what is defined as the Mass of St. Pius V. Sister Maria Pia Cecilia Manelli, Franciscan of the Immaculata, in her essay "Saint Francis, Advocate of the Roman Liturgy," published in the *Annales Franciscani*, 2009, shows with fine precision how the Missal promulgated by Pope Pius V in 1570, according to the directives of the Council of Trent, recalled the one in use among the Franciscans.

The text of the Missal upon which the reform by Pius V was based was the *Ordinarium Missae Secundum Consuetudinem Romanae Ecclesiae*, especially propagated by the Friars Minor, who had adopted for their newly founded order the Missal of the Papal Chapel.

Therefore, the scholar concludes at the end of a detailed historical reconstruction:

> Right after the promulgation of the 1570 Missal by St. Pius V—with the papal bull *Quo Primum,* ratifying the decisions of the Council regarding the Liturgy and codifying a liturgical tradition that in its essential part, the Canon, went back to the Apostles—the Franciscans enforced the use of that Missal to their whole religious order. [...] Ultimately, all they did was to reclaim the same Missal they had previously restructured and promoted.

Padre Pio and the Franciscans of the Immaculata: a return to the source

In close communion with the original Franciscan vocation, Padre Pio could love and venerate only the Mass he had always celebrated. That was the spring from which flowed all the graces that had filled his soul and that had to be the spring to draw upon for everyone willing to restore the true spirit of the founder.

It is not pure chance, then, but one of those precious tools used by Divine Providence, that the Institute of the Franciscans of the Immaculata, founded by Padre Stefano Maria Manelli, a spiritual son of the stigmatic saint, has linked the return to the Franciscan sources with the recovery of the ancient liturgy.

The history of this new branch of St. Francis's family goes back to the year 1965, when Padre Manelli, a Conventual Friars Minor, rediscovered and meditated upon the writings of the origins of the Order and those of St. Maximilian Kolbe, visited the early Franciscan places, and studied in depth the spiritual reflection of the seraphic family. Giuseppe Giuntella, in the essay "The Franciscans of the Immaculata in their Spiritual and Apostolic Dimension," *Annales Franciscani* 2006, writes:

> In Stefano grew more and more the desire to live as a true Franciscan who holds up the Lateran, by a life entirely spent at the service of the Church and for the Church. For this, on October 4, 1967, under the guidance of Padre Pio of Pietrelcina, he had the inspiration to consecrate himself with a special offering of himself to God through the Immaculata, for the necessities of the Church, thus anticipating and preparing the last step for the beginning of the history of a new foundation.

In Frigento, Avellino, on August 2, 1970, together with the co-founder Padre Gabriele M. Pellettieri, Padre Manelli brought to life the first nucleus of an institute which soon called together other vocations, men only at first, then also female vocations, the latter ones gathered in the Institute of the Franciscan Sisters of the Immaculata. All these calls to religious life were put at the service and under the protection of Mary Immaculate, to whom the friars and sisters, dressed in a gray-azure habit, made a vow of unlimited consecration.

Therefore, while all the religious orders and religious families which followed the deception of forming a new life along the wide road of senseless openness to the world become extinguished little by little, these children of Francis, on their way along the narrow path, continue even now to summon a large number of souls seeking evangelical perfection.

What most of all attracts so many young people who ask to be accepted into this institute? It is very simple. Giuntella tells us in his essay by describing in very few lines the life of the two founders:

> The early rise in the morning, the bed made of planks with no bedding, the cold of the mountains, the sandals on bare feet, the short-cut hair, the simple meals, and the intense prayer made of the life of the two friars a real scene worthy of the Franciscan Fioretti.

This is exactly the opposite of what the Franciscans of the same order of Padre Pio did during the same years by modifying the *Rules* in the delusional aim of conquering the youth of the culture of plenty.

The Sixties, the beginning of the end of religious life

The intense life of prayer, the hard life of penance, and the Mass of St. Francis and of the whole Church handed down till the time of Padre Pio: these are the sure methods to mold true Christians.

Not by chance, but here, too, because of another of those so precious chisels used by Divine Providence, the institute founded by a spiritual son of Padre Pio is the one that supports and propagates the celebration of the Mass of all times: it has adopted the Motu Proprio, *Summorum Pontificum* by Pope Benedict XVI. This choice certainly did not earn popularity for the Franciscans of the Immaculata from within the ecclesial setting, which operates on an unrestrained openness to the world. Theirs was a choice definitely against the grain, even if, in a normal world, it would be foolish to define as contradictory the attempt to act in obedience to the pope within the Church. Nevertheless, despite the fact that the majority of Catholics are infected by the virus of opposition to the Holy Father and to those who follow him, and despite the fact that this seems strange to the prophets hypnotized by eccentric and reformist readings of the signs of the times, young people seek those Franciscans of genuine medieval soul rather than those going after the allures of adult Catholicism.

After all, there is no way other than prayer, penance, and Mass to reinvigorate the religious orders in a crisis of identity and, by consequence, of vocations.

In the years from 1965 to 2005, the number of the Jesuits practically halved; the number of Friars Minor, Dominicans, Salesians, and Capuchins was reduced by at least one third. Padre Manelli said in his presentation at the conference *The Motu Proprio Summorum Pontificum, A Great Gift to the Church*:

> If the members of the religious orders were 329,799 in 1965, 40 years after the closing of the Council there were 214,903 left. About 115,000 members of the religious orders, more than one third of their total number, was lost during these 40 years of post-Council. In order to regain 115,000 religious members lost in only 40 years, we may need several centuries.

It was not difficult to guess the consequences of perverting the nature of the Mass. "Man," further explains Padre Manelli in his presentation,

> when consecrated and devoted totally to God, as he dies to the world to live in God, makes a sacrifice, a real holocaust. This kind of sacrifice, after the one of the Mass and of martyrdom, is the most perfect, the most accepted by God, and the most fruitful for time and eternity. And, indeed, in the religious state we can find all elements proper to the sacrifice of the altar, that is to say, oblation (at the Offertory), immolation (at Consecration), consummation of the victim (at Communion). [...]

Ludovico Colin asks: "What is a religious?" Padre Manelli answers: "He is a host." Another question: "What about the religious life?" Answer: "A mystical Mass. For every religious, in fact, making the three vows means to climb Calvary, to be crucified with Jesus."

Bad liturgy and bad doctrine

Again, Padre Pio, in his life and teachings, has lived and voiced these reflections, and thus it is not difficult to see what the Saint of Pietrelcina dreaded in the liturgical reform, at that time still sketchy. Padre Manelli, so many years after those warnings, observes that his spiritual father had seen correctly:

> The religious life, then, has suffered the negative influence of the *Novus Ordo* even more, because the religious life is most

of all a liturgical life. [...] A well-founded liturgy, solid and compact, is proven and guaranteed as such mostly by the vitality and fruitfulness of the monastic and religious life; and, in turn, a monastic and religious life which is solid and in fruitful growth confirms and guarantees in the most sure way the authenticity of the liturgy of the Mystical Body of Christ. On the contrary, a monastic and religious life in ruinous retreat as it is nowadays cannot testify to anything other than a liturgy lacking in consistency and vital strength. [...] It is a sad but real fact that, in the post-conciliar confusion, the religious—with rare exceptions—not only have suffered, but also have propagated among the faithful the liturgical distortions which in the last 40 years have been escalating exponentially. Moreover, together with such distortions, they have also spread doctrinal errors.

For this reason the Franciscans of the Immaculata are increasingly adopting the *Vetus Ordo*, the Mass loved by St. Francis. Nor is there need of many theories to explain the reasons why. It is sufficient to run quickly through the following considerations from some young friars, as quoted by Padre Manelli:

> The Mass of St. Pius V makes me strongly aware of being a priest, *in Persona Christi,* during the celebration of the Holy Sacrifice.
>
> In the Mass of St. Pius V you can easily be partaker in the event of the Passion and Death of Christ, hence it is no surprise that numerous saints shed warm tears during the reenacting of the sacrifice of the Cross.
>
> In the Mass of St. Pius V one experiences even the physical work (genuflections, bows, signs of the Cross, upward gazes, movements ...) with which the priest *conficit sacramentum* [confects the sacrament].
>
> It is easy to understand that in the Mass of St. Pius V, immersed in silence and recollection, one can reach much better experiences of the ecstasies and raptures, as we read in the biographies of many saints.

"Constantinian" Franciscans and "Cathar" Franciscans

These sons of St. Francis are placed in the second part of the chapter to show how they differ from those we have met earlier. A sharp and precise terminology for distinguishing them is provided by Sr. M. Cecilia Pia Manelli in the essay "Saint Francis, Advocate of the Roman Liturgy." Thus we discover that the Franciscans of the Immaculata can be defined as "Constantinians," because they look at the past in order to seek solid foundations, first of all at the Mass of all time. Whereas "Cathar" Franciscans are those "who make of the order of St. Francis a "puritan sect," aiming to "purify the Church of the dross of the liturgy of prehistory."

The two ways of being a Franciscan are absolutely irreconcilable with each other, so much so that one of the two can only be the fruit of error. This is the case for the "Cathar" Franciscans: an oxymoron on the theological as well as on the historical level. Sr. M. Cecilia Pia Manelli says:

> The Cathars, at the time of St. Francis, refused the Eucharist, because they saw in it a mixture of human and divine, spiritual and material, whereby the spiritual world would come into contact with the material world, the latter one being held by them as evil. The Cathar Franciscans in today's world fall into the same error: for them, all that counts is the spirit, not the outward appearance. Consequently, the purification takes place in all that refers to matter and exterior devotions. Regarding the intellectual, emotional, and practical promotion of the ancient liturgy, probably there is not much to be expected by those Franciscans who are more active (perhaps too much so?) in promoting and organizing marches for peace and ecumenical meetings (sometimes may be a little syncretic?), rather than in promoting the ancient liturgy.

Not by chance, the "Cathar" Franciscans are out in front in the fight, sometimes under cover, sometimes in the open, against the *Motu Proprio* of Pope Benedict XVI on the ancient liturgy.

They are in a fight against Rome and, as the Franciscan sister of the Immaculata explains, even against "their very identity as Franciscans." As a result

> . . . they deny not only the Missal used and compiled by the friars who preceded them centuries earlier, but also the same spirit of the seraphic Father Francis. The one against *Summorum Pontificum* will be in the end a battle for self-destruction, for the annihilation of their own charisma, born *sub ductu Ecclesiae*.[7] "All friars must be Catholic, must live and talk as Catholics. If anyone, then, in words or in actions will fall away from the Faith and the Catholic life without amend, let him be absolutely expelled from our fraternity" (*Decreed Rule*). These are the recommendations of the seraphic father St. Francis, more than ever relevant and terrible in today's world, if we consider the large mass of religious calling themselves "Friars Minor," who may have only kept the name of Catholics.

Unfortunately, Padre Pio's "Throw them out!" is still very appropriate today.

---

[7] Under the guidance of the Church.

PART TWO

THE ABUSE OF
THE ENEMY AND THE
CARESS OF GRACE

CHAPTER 1

The Devil Exists,
I Met Him

Padre Pio fights hand to hand with Satan,
whereas many theologians maintain that the prince of
this world is a fabrication now out of fashion

In 1912, for the umpteenth time, Padre Pio was sent back home from the monastery. His health was a disaster: vomiting, sudden perspirations, vertigo, high temperatures. In October 1911, the friar had been seen by Dr. Antonio Cardarelli in Naples. The doctor was clear: this young man's days are numbered, and he cannot undergo a long trip. Therefore, they decided to take him to the nearer convent in Venafro.

Padre Pio of Pietrelcina was a living crucifix. Pains never abandon him; his eyes had become so weak that he was allowed to substitute the reading of the daily Divine Office with the recitation of the rosary. The friar used to call this prayer "the weapon." He surely had a great need of it, as his days were a continuous fight. And he needed it most of all because his adversary was none other than Satan.

An infernal racket

A Catholic knows perfectly well that the devil is the true enemy of every man. The fight with the devil, then, is not reserved for mystics and saints or for very special individuals, the kind to which Padre Pio belonged.

107

But there is a fundamental difference between our daily conflict with the evil one, and the conflict in which the saint in San
Giovanni Rotondo was engaged. The struggle between Padre Pio
and the devil did not take place only in the secret of the conscience,
when one has to chase away temptations or practice virtues. No,
Padre Pio and the devil were fighting in the physical sense of the
word. But for the Padre the presence of Jesus, with whom he could
converse as with a friend and guardian who is always present and
powerful, was extraordinary medicine against this exceptional
manifestation of evil.

In 1912, when the Capuchin returned to Pietrelcina to recom-
pose himself a little bit, a horrible torment lingered with him, vex-
ing him in his soul and body. The fight against the demon occurred
daily, except on Wednesdays, the day of the week traditionally
consecrated to St. Joseph, *terror daemonum* [terror of demons].

The backdrop to this disquieting duel was the simple small
house where the friar lived. Rino Camilleri writes:

> In the two rooms he occupied in the village, often Jesus
> Himself, in the morning, lifted him up from the ground and
> placed him back on the bed, black and blue and bleeding, as
> he was left from the fight with the devils. The "Pucinari," the
> residents of Pietrelcina, never got used to the infernal racket
> coming from that house at night.

The skeptical Bishop

Just as darkness was falling upon earth the physical clash with
the evil one began for the young Capuchin. The clash took place
not only in Pietrelcina, but also when he lived in the monastery.
Continuously every night, according to the unanimous and con-
cordant testimonies of the often-terrorized confreres, horrifying
noises came from his cell. These commotions always ended up with
a deafening detonation, which made everything shake. This final
blast was caused, according to Padre Pio, by the devil, who, unable

to overcome him, "popped off"[1] because of his bitter dismay: The devil literally exploded with rage. At that point, the friars would overcome their fears and rush into the cell, finding their confrere so sweaty that they needed to change his clothes from head to foot.

One day, the Bishop of Ariano Irpino happened to visit the convent. As the time of the "fight" and usual bustles was approaching, the friars started showing signs of uneasiness, and the prelate wanted to know the reason for it. After the Capuchins explained the reason for so much fear, the bishop laughed, admonishing them: "What? Do you still believe in these things of the Middle Ages?" But his skepticism was soon destroyed: from the cell of Padre Pio the usual noises started, including the distinctive final boom. The bishop turned pale. He asked and obtained that a friar watch over him [the bishop] during the night. At the first light of dawn, the bishop left the monastery in a certain haste.

Bluebeard and his minions

As much as our rationalistic mentality may rebel, the testimonies are unanimous when relating the characteristics and the extent of this demonic disturbance. From the Capuchin friar's cell came inhuman shouts and screams, strong noises of objects smashed into the walls or knocked over onto the floor. One of the spiritual sons of Padre Pio, Antonio Pandiscia, explains that Padre Pio in person confirmed these perturbing events:

> The temptations and persecutions, the physical pains and spiritual torments would alternate with the consolations of Jesus. Only voices at first, then real apparitions.

Padre Pio wrote to his spiritual director:

> Bluebeard then, together with many of his peers, except on Wednesdays, never ceases to beat me, I would say, to death. But the Lord and the other celestial noble personalities reinvigorate all of me with their frequent visitations.

---

[1] Another instance of Padre Pio's colloquialism.

His conversations with Jesus also started at this time, especially after morning communion:

> Every morning He comes in me, and pours into my heart all the effusion of His goodness. I wish, if I could do so, wash with my blood those places where I scandalized so many souls. But, forever praise the mercy of Jesus. This merciful Jesus always asks me for love.

The saint's descriptions of the aggressions he endured from the devil are overwhelming:

> Bluebeard does not want to give up. He showed himself under almost every shape possible. For several days now he comes to visit me together with his minions all armed with sticks and iron contraptions, and what is worse, under his own shape. Who knows how many times he threw me off the bed, dragging me all over the room. But patience! Jesus, our Mom,[2] the little Angel, St. Joseph, and Father St. Francis are almost always with me.

These are words that reveal an uncommon ability to read even the most extraordinary events in a simply realistic and rigorously Catholic way. Everything fits and confirms to the tradition the Church teaches regarding these manifestations and about the realities that guide them. The devil has a monstrous and terrifying aspect and he acts as a compact legion, as we explicitly read in numerous pages of the Gospel. But, even if he beats and drags his victim all over the room, he is condemned to an inevitable defeat because Jesus, His Blessed Mother, together with St. Joseph, St. Francis, and the Guardian Angel, defend Padre Pio.

Astonishingly, this testimony comes not from some medieval chronicle nor from some excerpt by the Fathers of the desert, but from a man who lived during the same years of the Great War, by

---

[2] The unaffected, confidential style of Padre Pio is evident in his use of this loving term for the Blessed Mother.

One of the pages of the ascetical-mystical manuscript dedicated by Padre Pio to the "Dark Night." The sheets were obtained from (made of) opened envelopes, using their insides.

Dedication of Padre Pio on the title page of the work *Dark Night—Spiritual Canticle of St. John of the Cross.* The words of the Carmelite saint frequently inspired the ascetical and mystical meditations of Padre Pio. The text says:

"Take and read attentively and meditate. The angel of God be to you in all of these enterprises an inspiration, a support, and a guide."

The dedication of Padre Pio to a spiritual son:

"In assisting at Holy Mass, absorb all of yourself in the tremendous mystery that is taking place before your eyes: the redemption of your friendship and reconciliation with God."

P. Pio Cap.

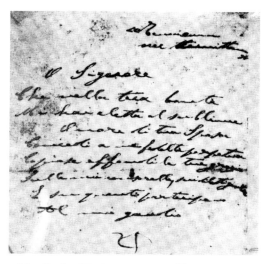

Prayer suggested by Padre Pio in memory of his sister Pia receiving of the habit: "*Tenui eum nec dimittum.*—[I held him and would not let go.]. O, Lord, who in your bounty / elected me to the sublime / honor of your spouse / concede to me perpetual faithfulness, / copious gifts of your grace / upon my sisters, their beloved parents, / and all of those involved / in my happiness."

Dedication of Padre Pio on the title page of the Missal of
Angelina Buratti, Venice (1958):

"In assisting at Holy Mass, renew your faith and
meditate upon the victim immolated for you to the
divine justice in order that it be placated and rendered
due propitiation.

"Do not remove yourself from the altar without
pouring out tears of sorrow and of love for Jesus
crucified for your eternal salvation. The Virgin of
Sorrows will provide you company and will be to you
sweet inspiration."

P. Pio Cap.

These unpublished photos from 1933 show Padre Pio finally returning to celebrate Mass publicly at the Convent of San Giovanni Rotondo after having been prohibited from publicly doing so during his first persecution.

Santa Maria degli Angeli Street in Pietrelcina. It was in this small room in the Forgione house that Padre Pio had undergone the most savage torments and assaults from the devil.

Padre Pio adoring the
consecrated Host.

Giuseppe Pagnossin with Padre
Pio in the sacristy of the convent
of San Giovanni Rotondo.

*The Madonna del Monte [Madonna of the Mountain] Appears
to Padre Pio*, in the sanctuary of Santa Maria del Monte in
Campobasso.

In this unpublished photo taken by Giuseppe Pagnossin during the
Mass of Friday September 20, 1968, the stigmata on Padre Pio's right
hand seems to have disappeared (noted particularly in the magnified
picture in the box). If this were so, the miraculous disappearance would
have occurred exactly 50 years after the initial imprinting of the sign of
crucifixion, which he had received on September 20, 1918, also a Friday.

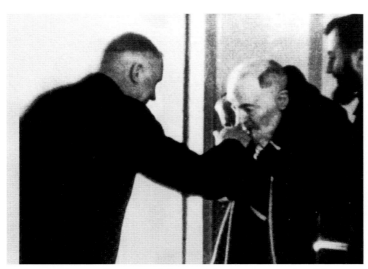

Padre Pio kisses the ring of the Archbishop Marcel Lefebvre, who
assisted at his Mass. It was found reported in the official bulletin from
the House of the Relief of the Suffering, dated March 31, 1967.

The First
Communion
of the daughter
of Giuseppe
Pagnossin.

Giuseppe Pagnossin
with Padre Pio.

Giuseppe Pagnossin and
his wife on the day of
their daughter's First
Communion, which she
received from Padre Pio.

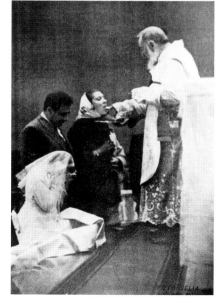

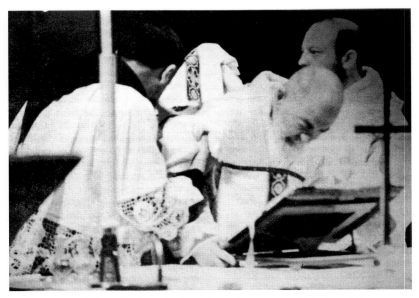

Padre Pio visibly suffering during the celebration of his last Mass, September 22, 1968. A few hours later he would be dead.

A view of the archives of the Society of Saint Pius X, where unpublished documents and autographs of Padre Pio, which had been left to Giuseppe Pagnossin, were recovered.

a witness of the Second World War, by a man who died in the year when the cultural revolution of the infamous "60s" broke out.

Padre Pio used to refer to the devil that tormented him with an expression that is all-explanatory: "That horrible thing." The quantity of epithets the saint used for the demon is almost innumerable. Padre Pio employed them many times in his letters sent from January 1911 to September 1915.

Reading the list of epithets produces an irresistible affection for this friar, so supernatural and at the same time so human: "ugly mustache bearer," "large mustache bearer," "bluebeard," "scoundrel," "wretched," "evil spirit," "horrible thing," "ugly rubbish," "ugly revolting animal," "unhappy junk," "ugly bad faces," "impure spirits," "those miserable ones," "wicked spirit," "ugly beast," "damned beast," "infamous apostate," "impure apostates," "gallows-faces," "roaring wild beasts," "spiteful tempter," "prince of darkness."

No doubt Padre Pio was a great saint, but also an excellent servant of the written Italian language, and just as much an awesome champion of humor. Thus come to life the many names to define the same horrible demonic reality. He narrates:

> I went through the other night very badly. That revolting thing from about ten o'clock, when I went to bed, until five o' clock in the morning, all he did was to beat me up continuously. He put into my mind many diabolical suggestions: thoughts of despair, of distrust in God. But praised be Jesus, because I defended myself by repeating to Jesus: *vulnera tua merita mea* [Your wounds, my merits].

Despite the sturdiest faith and the human tenaciousness that characterized him, the friar was led to think that those beatings would in time kill him and drive him insane:

> I really thought that it was for sure the last night of my life; or, if I did not die, I would lose my mind. But blessed be Jesus that none of this happened. At five o'clock in the morning, as soon as that ugly thing left, a sort of chill pervaded all of me, so that

I shivered from head to toe, like a reed exposed to a most violent wind. It lasted a couple of hours. I lost blood from my mouth.

A diabolical censorship

One of the most important objectives for the devil was to persuade Padre Pio to interrupt his correspondence with his spiritual father, so that he could isolate him completely and deprive him of the sure guide of an expert priest. Partly for this reason, and partly to spite Padre Pio, the demon often stained the letters from his spiritual directors, to make them unreadable. The letters would become legible only after they had been touched by the crucifix and sprinkled with holy water. Other times, the devil would try to prevent the young friar from reading the letters he had just received from his spiritual director.

In the winter of 1913, Padre Pio describes the phenomenon with the following words:

> Those ugly things lately, upon receiving your letter, before I opened it told me to shred it or to throw it into the fire. [...] I answered them that nothing would be able to make me change my mind. They hurled themselves at me like many starving tigers, cursing me and threatening me to make me pay for this. My father, they have kept their word! From that day on they have beaten me daily. But I am not terrified.

The tempter did not always use the same strategy: sometimes he tried to flatter his prey, courting him with good manners, but always ready to go back to the usual beatings when he realized his traps did not work.

The testimony of Padre Pio in this regard is an exceptional document for its contents and its narrative vigor. Perhaps very few writings by Christian mystics disclose with such precision the interaction which invisibly links us to the rebellious angel. All that Padre Pio saw and heard with his senses and with his own body is akin to the duel each one of us is compelled to live in the depth of the soul; some of us almost always ignore the ongoing duel, or, even openly deny the existence of the evil one. The extraordinary experience of this friar is a very precious lesson, valid for the most normal and ordinary human being.

> Quite the contrary, rather than getting scared, I got ready for the fight with a mocking smile on my lips toward them. Then for sure they showed themselves under the most abominable shapes; trying to make me cross the line, they started giving me the golden-glove treatment; but thanks to Heaven, I chastised them severely, handling them for what they are worth. And, as they saw all their efforts go up in smoke, they jumped on me, threw me onto the ground and hit me so hard, strewing pillows, books, chairs, all the while uttering desperate screams and pronouncing extremely filthy words.

In the winter of 1913, the torments had been going on for months, to the point that the young Capuchin was literally exhausted:

> By now 22 consecutive days are gone in which Jesus allows those ugly faces to give vent to their rage upon me. My body, my father, is all bruised because of so many beatings received at the hand of our enemies.

The "hard trade" of Padre Pio

Even though he was a saint, Padre Pio could not easily overcome the snares of the devil. The stigmatic friar had to fight with enormous strain, enduring moments of discouragement and facing the most dangerous temptation: despair. On May 18, 1913 he writes:

> I have been alone at night, alone during the day. A most harsh war began since that day with those ugly things. They pretended to make me think that God had rejected me at last.

For a gentle soul like his, this is the most terrible suggestion: to be persuaded by the deceit of the tempter to "displease Jesus,"

not to reciprocate His love. This is an often recurring theme in
the letters. Already in 1910, the friar wrote to his spiritual director:

> Regarding all of this [the impure temptations] I laugh as for
> futile things, following your advice. But I only grieve, at certain
> times, for not being sure if at the first attack of the enemy I was
> ready with prompt resistance.

Sometimes, during Spring of 1915, the defeat seemed to be sure:

> The fight against hell got to the point where I cannot go on
> any longer. […] The battle is exceptionally and extremely harsh;
> it seems like I may be capitulating at any time.

And further on:

> Truly, there are some moments, and these are not rare, when
> I feel as if squashed under the powerful strength of this awful
> monster. I really don't know where to turn; I pray, and many
> times the light is late in coming. What should I do? Help me, for
> charity's sake, do not abandon me. The enemies arise, oh father,
> non-stop against the small vessel of my spirit and all together
> shout at me: Let us knock him out, let us crush him, as he is
> weak and he cannot endure much longer. Alas! My father, who
> will free me from these roaring lions, all ready to devour me?

These pages clearly show what the life of this man was like.
They are also consolation for each one of us, because they show that
a saint is not a superman, is not a leading actor who plays a script
where the happy ending has already been written. He is not even
a spotless and unblemished hero, for whom the good completion
of any initiative is assured. The saint is a man like us, but he does
not make the mistake of engaging in a fight with the enemy and
thinking he is able to win with his own strength. Padre Pio was well
aware of these elementary Catholic truths, and he did not neglect
to synthetize this concept in one of his most famous witticisms. A

fellow confided to him: "Father, I want to be a saint." To which he replied: "My boy, you have chosen a hard trade."[3]

A very intelligent enemy

"My father," he again writes to the spiritual director in April 1915,

> I cannot take it anymore, I feel all my strength is abandoning me; the battle is truly at its last stage, any time now it seems like I am drowned by the waters of my tribulation. Alas! Who will save me? I am alone in the fight, day and night, against such a strong and powerful enemy. Who will prevail? To whom will victory smile? The fight is extreme on both sides, my father; taking stock of the respective strengths, I see myself weak, I see myself frail against the enemy's troops, I am about to be crushed, to be annihilated. Shortly, all things considered, it seems to me that the defeated one should actually be me. But what am I saying?! Is it possible that the Lord will allow this?! Never! I still feel raising, like a giant, in the inmost part of my spirit, the strength to cry out aloud to the Lord: "Save me, because I am about to perish."

From the writings of the Padre on the subject, we can strongly infer that the enemy acts with shrewdness and within a well-planned fight strategy.

> Satan with his evil ways never gets tired of engaging me in battle and storming my little fortress, by laying siege to it far and wide. In other words, Satan is for me like a powerful enemy, who, having resolved to take by force a town square, is not satisfied to assault it in one side or in a bastion, but he surrounds it from every side, assaults it everywhere at once, and torments it everywhere.

---

[3] It has already been noted that Padre Pio in his conversations often resorted to the common vernacular and displayed a ready wit. This is in sharp contrast to his writings, in which his style was always very meticulous and serious.

The diabolical manifestations against Padre Pio went on, with various intensity and frequency, throughout his life. Even in San Giovanni Rotondo the ugly things did not leave him alone.

In 1964, in the month of July at ten o'clock at night the Capuchins suddenly heard a heavy thump that made the floor shake. It came from Padre Pio's cell. Then they heard him cry: "Brothers, help me! Brothers, help me!" Quickly they ran to him and found him face down on the floor, bleeding from his forehead and from his nose, with a serious wound on his right eyebrow. It was necessary to apply two stitches to close the wound. On that day, the Padre had passed by a woman possessed by the devil; she was from a village in the area of Bergamo. The following day, the demon, from the mouth of the possessed woman, would acknowledge that at 10 pm of the previous day, he had paid a visit to someone, and he had taken revenge: "This will be a lesson for the next time..." For several days after this, the swollen face of the Padre showed the signs of his violent fight with that demon.

Crosses are like hair

The stigmata imprinted for almost 60 years on his body, the beatings of the demon, and all of the calumnies and persecutions show that the story of Padre Pio contains an impressive bundle of suffering, which the friar accepted with a spirit of endurance that astonishes and at the same time moves us.

After all, nothing happens by chance. The life of Padre Pio was one of integral Catholicism, with no short cuts, but was rock-solid and founded on the traditional doctrine of the Church and focused on the mystery of the death on the Cross of the Son of God. The "teachers" of Francesco Forgione had, as much as possible, "trained" him for this daily *Via Crucis*. Padre Benedetto of San Marco in Lamis, his spiritual director, had written in a booklet dedicated to Christian souls: "Crosses are like hair: as soon as you cut them they grow again."

Padre Pio endured, but always resorted to prayer and to all supernatural help. When he came across the sorrow of other people, he comforted them by saying: "Those tears of yours have been collected by the angels. They have been placed in a golden chalice. You will find them again when you will appear in front of God." In the writings of this saint we find words that have lost nothing of their freshness and their validity: "The pain endured separated from the Cross is unbearable," Padre Pio explains, "but, how gentle and bearable it becomes if one suffers not far from the Cross of Jesus."

> The friar with the stigmata also writes that pain is not a goal, but a means of expiation: I do not love suffering *per se*. I request it from God, I long for it because of the fruits it gives me: it gives glory to God, saves my brothers in this our exile, and frees the souls from the fire of Purgatory. What more should I wish for? The father chastises the children he loves. Do you know the proverb "Spare the rod, spoil the child"? God punishes because He loves us, He tries our love and our fidelity to make us worthy of His love and of Paradise.

And again:

> It is not suffering, but knowing how to suffer that counts. The former is for everyone, the latter is for a few. If you endure your illness with a spirit of acceptance you will gain many merits for yourself and your loved ones.

Someone must return to Calvary

Padre Pio had to bear the distressing presence of suffering and the bloody fight practically all his life. To the point that a great cardinal of last century, Giuseppe Siri, asked himself:

> A man who stays crucified for half a century? What does this mean? Do you know why Jesus went on the Cross? He went on the Cross because of men's sins, and when, in history, we see someone crucified[...]it means that the sins of men are big and to save them it is necessary for someone to return to Calvary,

climb again on the Cross, and stay there to suffer for his brothers. Our times need people who offer what the Only Begotten Son suffered. [...] Here is the whole story of Padre Pio.

On February 13, 1913, the friar himself wrote these disturbing words addressed to him by Jesus:

> Do not worry, I will have you suffer, but I will also give you the strength to endure it. I desire that your soul by a daily and hidden martyrdom be purified and tested; do not be scared if I allow the demon to torment you, the world to disgust you, the people to you most dear to afflict you, because nothing will prevail against those who moan under the Cross for love of me and whom I have labored to protect. How many times you would have abandoned me, my son, if I had not crucified you. Under the Cross you learn how to love, and I will not give it to everyone, but only to the souls most dear to Me.

Never lower your guard

Some confreres narrate that some days Padre Pio used to spend time with them on the little terrace of the monastery, after spending many hours in the confessional. This for him was a moment of relaxation. He used to talk about life in the monastery, about world events, but he framed everything in the light of God. He used to say: "My children, be prudent and watchful, never lower your guard, because the devil is always ready to hit us. Do you see the wall of the cloister?" and in saying so he would turn his gaze beyond the railing of the little terrace. Then, continuing: "How many little devils are there crouched waiting to come into the monastery and tear us to pieces!...Don't forget!"...And with a concerned paternal look he would hug the confreres, as if to shield them from the enemy. Then he used to add: "Also the Church, that is our mother and that I love with all my being, must defend itself from many enemies. Let us pray especially for the pope! May the Holy Spirit always enlighten him!"

A very strange penitent

One morning Padre Pio was hearing confessions as usual. At one point, a gentleman, tall, slim, rather elegantly dressed, and of polite and gentle manners, entered the confessional. After kneeling down, the stranger began the accusation of his faults. They were against God, against neighbors, against morals. All of them were revolting. Later, Padre Pio talked about this episode to Padre Tarcisio of Cervinara:

> One thing struck me. Regarding every one of his accusations, even after my rebuke made by citing as witness the word of God, the magisterium of the Church, and the moral of the saints, this enigmatic penitent rebutted my words, justifying with extreme ability and with very polished gentleness, any kind of sin, emptying it of any malice and trying at the same time to show all the sinful actions as if they were normal, natural, humanly indifferent. This was not only regarding the horrific sins against God, Jesus, the Blessed Mother, the saints, whom he addressed using irreverent circumlocutions without ever naming them, but also regarding sins which were morally so filthy and loutish to touch the bottom of the most nauseating sewer.

This story is even more frightful than those of the beatings and physical fights with the devil. Our times are dominated by people "rather elegantly dressed and of polite manners" who constantly strive to demolish the traditional morals and justify and make normal any sort of sin. Who, then, governs this period of human history? But it is better to hear the rest of the story in the saint's own words:

> The answers that this enigmatic penitent gave from time to time to my argumentations, with skillful subtlety and muffled malice, shocked me. I was asking myself the questions: "Who is this person? Where does he come from? Who can he possibly be?" And I tried to take a good look at his face in order to read something amid the wrinkles of his face; at the same time I sharpened my hearing at each one of his words so that none of

them could escape my attention in order to weigh them in all their reach. At a certain point, by a vivid and bright interior light, I clearly perceived who was in front of me. So with a decisive and imperious tone I told him: "Say 'Praise to Jesus, hail to Mary.'" As soon as I pronounced these most delightful and most powerful names, Satan disappeared instantly in a blazing flame, leaving behind him an unbearable and suffocating stink.

The vision of 1903

At this point it is necessary to let Padre Pio talk a little bit more at length, because in this regard there is nothing more accurate than what he was allowed to know in three visions between January 1 and January 5, 1903. The first vision displayed to him all the coming days of his life as a continuous fight against the demon, and it was decisive in making him resolve to "say farewell to the world and dedicate oneself entirely to God within a sacred cloister." The second vision explained clearly to him the meaning of what he had learned from the previous one. The third vision, during the night before he set out for the monastery of Morcone, was exclusively one of consolation and encouragement for him from Jesus and Mary.

In nomine Iesu [In the name of Jesus]. *Amen.*
Everything which I am about to relate in this poor account is set down in virtue of holy obedience. God alone can fully understand the great repugnance with which I write these things. He alone is my witness, and if he had not greatly strengthened me in the respect due to authority, I should have resolutely refused to the point of rebellion and should never have been induced to set down what I am about to write, fully aware as I am of the wickedness of this soul which was favored by Heaven with such signal graces. May God be pleased to help and strengthen me, so that I may overcome the confusion I experience in manifesting what I am about to relate.

Here is the first extraordinary call to this soul, in order that he should leave the world and the path to his own damnation, and devote himself entirely to God's service.

This soul had felt strongly from his earliest years the vocation to the religious state, but as he grew older, alas, he began to drink great draughts of this world's vanity. In the heart of this poor creature, a powerful battle began between the increasingly strong vocation on the one hand and a sweet but false delight in the things of the world on the other. Perhaps, or rather, without a doubt, with the passage of time the feelings would have triumphed over the spirit and would have smothered the good seed of the divine call. But the Lord who desired this soul for himself was pleased to favor this person with the vision I am about to describe.

While he was meditating one day on his vocation and wondering how he could make up his mind to bid farewell to the world in order to devote himself entirely to God in a holy enclosure, his senses were suddenly suspended and he was made to gaze with the eye of his intellect on things quite different from those seen by bodily eyes:

He beheld at his side a majestic figure of rare beauty, radiant as the sun. This man took him by the hand and he heard him say: "Come with me, for it is fitting that you fight as a valiant warrior." He led him to a vast plain, where there was a great multitude of people, divided into two groups. On one side he saw men of beautiful countenance, clad in snow-white garments; on the other, in the second group, were black-robed men of hideous appearance who seemed like dark shadows.

Between these two large groups was a wide space in which that soul was placed by his guide. As he gazed intently at the two groups, suddenly in the middle of that space which separated them a man advanced, so tall that his forehead touched the clouds, while his countenance was that of a hideous black monster.

At this sight the poor soul was completely disconcerted and felt his life suspended. The strange figure advanced nearer and the guide at the side of that soul informed him that he would have to fight this individual. At these words the poor thing turned pale, trembled all over and was on the point of falling to the ground in a faint, so great was the terror he experienced.

The guide supported him with one arm until he had recovered somewhat from his fright. The soul then turned to his guide and begged him to save him from the fury of that strange being, because, he told him, that man was so strong that the strength of all men combined would not be sufficient to knock him down.

"All resistance is useless; it is advisable that you fight this man. Take heart; enter confidently into the combat, go forward courageously, for I shall be close to you. I will assist you and not allow him to overcome you. In reward for your victory over him, I'll give you a splendid crown to adorn your head."

The poor soul took heart and entered into combat with that dreadful and mysterious being. The impact was tremendous, but with the aid of his guide, who never left his side, he finally overcame his adversary, threw him to the ground and obliged him to flee.

Then the guide, faithful to his promise, took from beneath his robes a crown of exceptional splendor, of indescribable beauty, which he placed on his head. But after an instant he withdrew the crown, saying as he did so: "I shall reserve for you an even more beautiful crown if you succeed in the combat with that being with whom you have already fought. He will return continually to the attack to regain his lost honor. Fight valiantly and have no doubt about my assistance. Keep your eyes wide open, for that mysterious being will endeavour to take you by surprise. Don't be afraid of his attacks or of his dreadful aspect. Remember what I have promised you: that I'll always be close to you and help you so that you'll always succeed in overcoming him."

When that mysterious being had been vanquished, the entire multitude of hideous men took to flight with shrieks and imprecations and deafening cries, while from the other multitude came the sound of applause and praise for the splendid man more radiant than the sun who had assisted the poor soul so magnificently in the fierce combat. Here the vision ended.

This vision filled that poor soul with such great courage that it seemed like a thousand years before he was able to abandon the world forever, to devote himself entirely to God's service in a religious institute.

The vision just described was understood by that soul, although not quite clearly. The Lord, however, was pleased to manifest the meaning of this symbolic vision to him by a further one a few days before he entered religion. I say a few days earlier, because he had already applied to the Provincial Superior for admission and had received an affirmative reply, when the Lord granted him this further vision which was purely intellectual.

This occurred on the Feast of Our Lord's Circumcision, five days before he was to leave his home. He had received Holy Communion and was engaged in intimate converse with his Lord when his soul was suddenly flooded with supernatural light. By means of this most pure light he understood in a flash that his entry into religion in the service of the heavenly King meant being exposed to combat with that mysterious being from hell with whom he had fought in the previous vision.

He then understood, and this was sufficient to hearten him, that although the demons would be present at his battles to make fun of his failures, on the other hand there was nothing to fear, because the angels would also be present to applaud his victories over Satan.

Both were symbolized by the two groups he had seen in the previous vision. He also understood that although the enemy he had to fight was a terrible one, he had no reason to be afraid, because Jesus Christ Himself, represented by that radiant person who had acted as his guide, would assist him, would always be at his side to help him and would reward him in paradise for the victories achieved, provided he place his trust in him alone and fight generously.

This vision made that soul strong and generous in bidding farewell to the world. However, it must not be imagined that he had nothing to suffer in the lower part of his soul as he abandoned his own family to whom he was strongly attached. He felt even his bones being crushed as this leave-taking approached and the pain was so intense that he almost fainted.

As the day of his departure drew nearer, this anguish increased. On the last night he spent with his family, the Lord came to console him by yet another vision. He beheld in all their majesty Jesus and His Blessed Mother, who encouraged him and assured him of their predilection. Finally, Jesus placed a hand on his head and this was sufficient to strengthen the higher part of his soul, so that he shed not a single tear at this painful leave-taking, although at that moment he was suffering agonies in soul and body.[4]

The friar from Apulia[5] and the theologian from Germany

Padre Pio died on September 23, 1968. But 37 years later, the cardinals, gathered in conclave, elected Joseph Cardinal Ratzinger, prefect of the Congregation of the Doctrine of Faith, to be the next pope. These two men were very different from each other: a Samnite[6] and a German, a friar little inclined to preaching and a theologian quite used to speaking in public, a symbol of popular devotion and someone considered by his detractors cold and detached from the people.

Nonetheless, these two men have more things in common than the superficial observer may imagine. For instance, both of them believe that the devil exists. Nice discovery, somebody may say: they are both Catholics. But nowadays, this cannot be taken so much for granted. Padre Pio was regularly encountering the devil, even if he would have rather avoided meeting those "monsters" almost every day. Certainly, never, ever would he have doubted the existence of the rebellious angel who, again and again, tempted even Our Lord.

Obviously, the devil is the signal object of mockery preferred by atheists, unbelievers, and the enemies of the Church. But even among Catholics, especially among the educated and wise, among

---

[4] Padre Pio of Pietrelcina: *Letters*, tr. Padre Gerardo Di Flumeri (Our Lady of Grace Capuchin Friary Editions, 2nd edition, San Giovanni Rotondo, Italy, 1984), Vol. 1 1910-1922, pp. 1426-1428.

[5] Apulia is the south-easternmost region of Italy.

[6] From the old Roman province of Samnium, covering an area corresponding to the present day central Italian provinces of Benevento, Isernia, and Campobasso.

theologians and experts, there is no lack of those who, upon hearing about the devil, smile with an attitude of forbearance.

Joseph Cardinal Ratzinger, though he was a man of eclectic culture, does not think as they do. In 1985, in an interview by Vittorio Messori in *Rapporto sulla fede*,[7] Cardinal Ratzinger says at one point:

> Whatever some superficial theologians may say, the devil is, for the Christian faith, a mysterious presence, but real, personal, not a symbolic one. It is also a powerful reality ("the prince of this world," (Mt. 9:34); (Jn. 12:31); the New Testament repeatedly mentions his existence), an evil superhuman free being that opposes the liberty of God, as a realistic reading of human history demonstrates, with its abyss of atrocities always renewed and impossible to explain by man alone.

Here we have a Samnite friar and a German theologian, a priest in a small Italian monastery and a cardinal destined to become pontiff. They, in different ways, teach the same thing by reiterating with theological correctness that the Christian has as his main enemy the demon and as invincible armor the Cross of Christ. This was clearly demonstrated by Pope Benedict XVI during his visit to San Giovanni Rotondo on June 21, 2009 when he spoke about the stigmatic saint in his homily:

> As it was for Jesus, the true fight and the fundamental combat Padre Pio had to endure were not against earthly enemies, but against the spirit of evil (Eph. 6:12). The biggest tempests that threatened him were the assaults of the devil, from which he defended himself with God's armor, with the "shield of Faith," and "the sword of the Spirit, which is the Word of God" (Eph. 6:11, 16-17). By remaining united to Jesus, he always focused on the depth of the human drama, and for this he offered himself and offered his many pains; and he was able to devote himself to the cure and relief of the sick, the privileged sign of God's

---

[7] Joseph Cardinal Ratzinger with Vittorio Messori, *The Ratzinger Report* (Ignatius Press, San Francisco, CA, 1987).

mercy; of His Kingdom to come, rather than that which is already in the world; of the victory of love and life over sin and death. His was to guide the souls and lighten the suffering: thus, we can summarize the mission of Saint Pio, as the servant of God, Pope Paul VI, said of him: "He was a man of prayer and suffering" (*To the Capuchin Chapter Fathers*, February 20, 1971).

All of this holds because Padre Pio was a man of the Cross, said the Pontiff.

A simple man, of humble origins, "apprehended by Christ" (Phil. 3:12)—as the Apostle Paul says of himself—to make of him a chosen instrument of the everlasting power of His Cross, a power of love for the souls, of forgiveness and reconciliation, of spiritual paternity, and of effective solidarity with the suffering. The stigmata that marked him on his body united him intimately with the Crucified-Resurrected One. As an authentic follower of St. Francis of Assisi, he took upon himself, like the Poverello,[8] the experience of the Apostle Paul, as the Apostle describes it in his Letters: "With Christ I am nailed to the Cross. And I live, now not I; but Christ liveth in me" (Gal. 2:19-20); or else, "So that death worketh in us, but life in you" (Cor. 4:12). This is not a sign of alienation, loss of personality: God never annihilates the human, but reshapes it with His Spirit and directs it at the service of His plan of salvation. Padre Pio kept his natural gifts and also his temperament, but offered everything to God, who could make use of it freely to extend the work of Christ: announcing the Gospel, forgiving sins, and healing the sick in body and spirit.

How can one follow the example of such an imitator of Christ, at war with the devil and nailed on the Cross? Pope Benedict XVI explains:

First of all, prayer. Like all the great men of God, Padre Pio had become himself a prayer, body and soul. His days were a liv-

---

[8] Literally "the poor little one," a name by which St. Francis came to be known.

ing rosary, that is to say, a continuous meditation and assimilation of the mysteries of Christ in spiritual unity with the Virgin Mary. This is the explanation of the singular presence in him of both supernatural gifts and human reality. And all of this had its apex in the celebration of the Holy Mass.

CHAPTER 2

Save Us From
The Fires of Hell…

> Padre Pio says that we must consider with great seriousness
> the *Novissimi*, and he shows a great and loving devotion for
> the souls in Purgatory.

Certainly Padre Pio is not the only saint in the history of
the Church who manifested a special devotion for the souls in
Purgatory. To pray for the dead is a characteristic attribute of
Catholicism, and only from the 1900s on, did beliefs of Lutheran
and Protestant origin spread within the Church, aiming at the
denial of the existence of Purgatory.

The Sisters of the Souls in Purgatory

Some saints have even chosen the task of praying for the holy
souls in Purgatory as the fundamental gift or inspiration of the
congregations they founded. This, for example, was what Blessed
Francesco Faà of Bruno did. Born in Alessandria in 1825, the last
of 12 children, he had been a valiant officer of the Piedmontese
army.[1] Precisely while in the military, during the bloody battle
of Novara, he, a fervent Catholic, saw thousands of young men
go to their death in battle, and knew not whether they were in
the state of grace or not. These were thousands of souls in danger
of eternal punishment, or of languishing in Purgatory forgotten
by everyone. For this reason, Francesco Faà of Bruno decided to

---

[1] Piedmont is a region in Northwest Italy where the Royal House of Savoy resided
before becoming the Italian monarchs.

129

found the Minim Sisters of Our Lady of the Suffrage, with the specific task to pray every day for the souls in Purgatory. "Pray, act, suffer" was the motto of this scientist, inventor, architect, and genius, disliked by the ruling class of the Piedmont because of his Catholicism, which exhibited no short cuts or compromises with the ruling masonic elite. His motto was one which Padre Pio would have also liked very much.

The two men had much in common: For instance, their name: Francis, for both were named after St. Francis of Paola. They also shared a great love for the souls of the deceased, who are waiting for our prayers to free them from their suffering.

After all, Catholic doctrine teaches that there are three categories of men constituting the one and only Church: the Church triumphant, made of all the souls who are in Paradise already; the Church suffering, that is to say, the souls who need to be purified before admittance to their beatitude; and the Church militant, composed of those who are not yet dead and struggle for the salvation of their soul. Once this three-fold structure gets set aside, Purgatory is the first of the three to be eliminated.

The Mass and the Suffering Souls in Purgatory

Padre Pio did not waste his time doubting the sanity of traditional Catholic doctrine, and he prayed ardently for the dead saved from damnation though not yet ready for the beatific vision of God. The Padre used to say that his intention was to "empty Purgatory" one step at a time, reciting one rosary after another.

Padre Pio always remembered the holy souls in Purgatory, not only in his daily prayers, but, most of all, in the holy sacrifice of the Mass: at the time of the *Memento* for the dead, Padre Pio always paused at length to pray for the deceased souls. His meditation during this part of the Mass could last, according to the most reliable testimonies, even 15 minutes. Padre Alessio Parente, a Franciscan who lived close to Padre Pio, had written that in all of the Capuchin monasteries, in the place most often frequented by the majority of the friars, there was on the wall a framed inscription with an invitation to remember and to pray for the souls in Purgatory; the inscription read: "An easy and fast way to make amends for the souls in Purgatory." In it was a list of the categories of souls in need. In a small wooden box next to, or below, the frame there were dice with numbers matching the categories of the souls in Purgatory listed. This way, anyone who passed by tossed a die and recited a prayer for the related category of souls.

Viva[2] Padre Pio!

One day, while chatting with some friars who asked him about the importance of praying for these souls, the Padre made a striking statement: "On this mountain of San Giovanni Rotondo more souls in Purgatory than living men and women climb to participate in the Masses I celebrate and to seek my prayers."

One evening, in the middle of the Second World War, after the evening meal, while the doors of the monastery were already closed for the night, the friars heard voices coming from the entrance, crying: "Viva Padre Pio!"

The Father Superior at that time, Padre Raffaele of Sant'Elia a Pianisi, called the porter, Friar Gerardo of Deliceto, and ordered him to see what was going on, and, because it was so late, to send away the people who had entered the monastery. Friar Gerardo obeyed. But when he reached the entrance hall, he found everything in place, all lights were off, and the entrance door well secured by the two metal rods blocking it. Then he made a short inspection of the adjacent rooms and reported to Father Superior the findings of his inspection.

Everyone had distinctly heard the voices, and the Superior remained perplexed. The next morning, he decided to seek clari-

---

2 "Viva," literally "Long live," is an exclamation used to express public acclaim: it is a mix of "Long live," "Hail," "More power to," "Praise to," and the like.

fication from Padre Pio himself. The stigmatic friar, giving little importance to the matter, and, speaking calmly, as if the occurrence were the most common and ordinary thing in the world, reassured the Superior: the voices which had screamed "*Viva Padre Pio*" belonged to some dead soldiers who had come to thank him for his prayers.

The flames of Purgatory

One day, one of his confreres, a Capuchin from the province of Foggia who was not a priest, Brother Modestino of Pietrelcina, asked the Padre: "Padre, what do you think of the flames of Purgatory?" He said in return: "If the Lord were to allow the soul to go from that flame to the hottest fire on earth, it would be like going from boiling water into fresh water."

Purgatory was something that Padre Pio knew well. He spoke about it not by hearsay or because he had read about it in books, but he spoke from his personal experience. One day Brother Joseph Longo of San Giovanni Rotondo, a brother not a priest, went to Padre Pio to ask for his prayers for a young sick woman confined to a wheelchair, unable to walk.

Brother Joseph knelt down, as he used to, and absent-mindedly placed his knees right on the wounded feet of Padre Pio, who almost screamed because of the pain. Then, after the cause of the trouble was removed, with affection he told his fellow brother, who was much afflicted: "It is as if you made me go through ten years of Purgatory!"

A few days later Brother Joseph went to pay a visit to the family of that young woman to reassure her that he had accomplished the mission of notifying Padre Pio of their request and that he would pray for her. He found out then that the girl had started walking on the same day he had knelt on the feet of Padre Pio.

One day the Padre was asked: "Padre, what can I do to suffer my pains of Purgatory here on earth so that I will go afterward straight to Heaven?" The Padre answered: "By accepting everything from the hands of God, by offering to Him everything with love and thanksgiving. Only in this way can we go from our death bed straight to Paradise."

Padre Pio often explained to the faithful that it was not only necessary to pray for the souls of the departed ones, but that it was necessary to know how much they pray for us, and how precious their unceasing prayer is. "It is more acceptable to God," said the friar,

> ... the prayer of those who suffer and who, while suffering, ask God for graces for the good of others. The prayer of the souls in Purgatory is much more efficacious in the eyes of God because they are in a state of suffering, a suffering for love of God, to whom they aspire, and for the neighbor, for whom they pray.

But of what kind is this suffering experienced in Purgatory? Certainly, the lot of the suffering souls is not a comfortable one: it is not as if they were simply in a large waiting room where it is only a matter of being patient. As in hell, the pain is of two kinds: one consisting in the deprivation of God; the other, in the afflicting pain, in the punishment that harms and provokes real pain. Many saints have equated the pains of Purgatory with those in Hell: Saint Catherine of Genoa talks about "torments that cannot even be described in words, and of which human intelligence cannot have the slightest idea." St. Thomas Aquinas believed that the flames in these two places were of the same kind. This belief is indeed confirmed by Padre Pio, who once told Cleonice Morcaldi: "My daughter, in some places Purgatory is the same as Hell."

Protecting the souls from heresies

In summary, Padre Pio did not mince words, not even when he faced his superiors. If truth needed to be said, the Saint of Pietrelcina had no problem. Nor could he be intimidated by respect for the fashions or the prevailing mindset. Thus, even if he lived in an environment becoming more and more skeptical every day regarding the existence of Purgatory, he did not take even one step back, but continued to pray and ask for prayers for the souls waiting for the go-ahead into Heaven.

After all, he knew well that the roots of that denial were old, going back to the Protestant Revolt. In his hand-written notebook can be found unequivocal expressions regarding Protestantism and its "noble fathers," expressions that nowadays would embarrass many dyed-in-the-wool ecumenists, according to whom all Christian beliefs are equivalent. Padre Pio writes:

> Now, no other group, separated from the Roman Church, has the mark of sanctity in any way. First, because they have no founders other than Luther, Calvin, and people of their kind, full of pride, filled to the brim with vices; they separated from the Church to follow their evil passions by which they were subjugated.

However, the saint adds, the problem does not reside only in the unworthiness of the founders. The trouble is that "the doctrine these sects teach is ungodly and immoral." In fact, they teach that

> ...it is lost time, rather sacrilegious, to have recourse to the intercession of the saints, and especially of the Most Holy Mother, and that their images must be stepped on and thrown into the fire; and that faith alone is sufficient to be saved, therefore blasphemy, immodesty, sacrilege are not impediments to the salvation of man, as long as he believes.

Padre Pio, like the majority of his contemporaries, had studied well the essential teachings of Catholic doctrine; therefore it was quite natural for him to draw the due conclusions.

I died in 1908

Padre Pio had a very special intimacy with the souls in Purgatory. From his writings and from the testimonies of those who lived with him, come dozens upon dozens of encounters which are completely extraordinary for us, but nonetheless were experienced with absolute normality by the Padre.

One evening Padre Pio was in the monastery by the fireplace.

> I was praying with my eyes closed, when I saw the door open and an old man, wrapped in a cloak in the fashion of the peasants of San Giovanni Rotondo, came in and sat beside me. I looked at him but I did not ask myself how he could have entered the monastery at that time of the evening. I addressed him and asked: "Who are you? What do you want? He answered: Padre Pio, I am Pietro Di Mauro, son of the late Nicola nicknamed Precoco."[3]

Then he added:

> I died in this monastery on September 18, 1908, in cell no. 4, at the time when they used to shelter the poor. One evening, while I was in bed, I fell asleep with my cigar lit, which set fire to my straw mattress, and I died suffocated and burned. I am still in Purgatory. I need one Holy Mass to be freed. The Lord allowed me to come and ask for help.

After listening to him, I answered:

> Be reassured, tomorrow I will celebrate the Holy Mass for your liberation.

The friar, of course, did just that with the usual devotion. His confreres, informed about this episode, went to gather some information in the village, and every detail regarding the poor Pietro Di Mauro, son of the late Nicola, was confirmed.

Hey boy, did you say Mass?

Well, then: whether we speak of the living or the dead, whether we pray to obtain a grace or to help a soul in Purgatory, at the end we always come back to the starting point in the life of the

---

[3] Dialect for "peach."

Christian: the Mass. The Mass that Padre Pio put at the center of his day, preparing for it with an uncommon devotion, celebrating it with a slowness filled with participation in the mystery of Christ's suffering, and then thanking Him at the end for almost one hour, as if every Mass were the first and last in his life.

Also, on the day of his death Padre Pio showed himself concentrated in a fixed way on this ineffable mystery. It was one night in September 1968 when the friar realized that the uninterrupted suffering of his earthly life was coming to an end. Then he asked his friars to stay close to him, holding hard the hand of Padre Pellegrino, who used to take care of him. Concerned, he asked his confreres that a Mass be celebrated for him. Padre Pio of Pietrelcina, at birth Francesco Forgione, who had spent all his life asking for prayers and celebrating Masses for the holy souls in Purgatory, now asked, insistently, the same thing for his soul.

At one point, addressing Padre Pellegrino, he told him: "Hey, you, boy, did you say Mass?"

The friar answered: "Spiritual Father, it is too early now to say Mass."

And Padre Pio in reply: "Well, this morning you will offer Mass for me."

CHAPTER 3

God Exists, I Met Him

Padre Pio is the instrument thanks to which
the Lord brings back the lost sheep to the fold
and converts them to a new life

Fifteen, sixteen, sometimes even nineteen hours a day, the
Padre spent between the altar and the confessional. The work pace
of Padre Pio in the Lord's vineyard was impressive. He got up every
day at 3:30 am, then went down to the small church to make the
appropriate preparation for Mass which began at five. It seems that
the predawn Mass time had been explicitly requested by the young
friar, in order to allow the peasants to attend before heading to the
fields. It has been estimated that a total of 20 million people had
attended the Mass celebrated by Padre Pio.

When the liturgy was over, he used to proceed to the other one
of his fundamental occupations: the souls of sinners. Except for
pauses for meals and personal prayer, this was for him practically
a nonstop engagement. About five million people would go to his
confessional throughout the years. The requests were so numerous
that, at a certain point, an office was instituted in charge of regu-
lating the flow of the penitents using an appropriately numbered
ticket.

Padre Pio never participated in a "meeting for the organization
of the pastoral plan for the community," never followed a "course
for the leadership of the oratory," and never organized even one
session of the "parochial pastoral council." Instead, he spent hours
and hours in the confessional. That was the place where people
were looking for him and wanted him. To find him, one had to

go to that mysterious physical place, where the most diverse souls gather to unload the multitude of their sins and leave cleansed by the forgiveness of Christ.

What sin Is

The extraordinary availability of Padre Pio in welcoming the penitents to the confessional originated, first of all, from his simple compliance with his duty of state. The friar with the stigmata was a Catholic priest of sane and healthy Tridentine formation and knew that there are specifically two things that only the priest can do: celebrate Mass and give the absolution for sins. No lay person, even the most saintly and devout in the world, can substitute for a priest in these two extraordinary responsibilities. Padre Pio had understood this, and he literally allowed himself to be "devoured" by the Christian people, who tortured him in order to be able to receive the sacrament from him and, not rarely, spiritual direction and some practical advice. Just like a multitude of priests and religious had done during the long history of the Church, he too submitted himself to this very wearing marathon of patience and of mercy.

Undoubtedly, his was a very personal style, and nowadays it would leave dumbfounded more than one expert in "the pastoral of reconciliation." The Capuchin Saint did not refrain from using strong manners with certain penitents. It is well known that, in some cases, he reached the point of refusing absolution, or of using harsh words with the faithful who tried to act smart with him and, especially, with the Eternal Father. This happened only because the Padre did not wish any of the little sheep in his care to be lost.

Most of all, there was in him the absolute ability to perceive the gravity of sin, and of every sin, in his penitents. Padre Eusebius Notte says that one time, Padre Pio wanted to go to confession to him, who was then a very young friar priest. His opposition was soon overcome by his older confrere, as he started reciting the *Confiteor*, Padre Eusebio recounts:

Sin is the betrayal of love [handwritten annotation]

After the declaration of his sins, something happened that deeply bewildered me: Padre Pio broke down in a copious weeping. To console him, I tried to tell him that it was not at all necessary, given the lightness of his faults. At that point he intervened: "My son, you, too, think that sin is the transgression of a law. No! Sin is the betrayal of love. What did the Lord do for me, and what do I do for Him?"

The Confessional

The stigmatic friar used to meet that unceasing flux of penitents in a traditional, honest confessional of the old style: a wooden structure in the middle of which the priest sits, and on each of the two sides kneel, beyond a grid, the faithful. In general, this was the setting for Padre Pio: these little "huts of forgiveness" have a peculiarity that few people notice: the two slopes of the little "roof" above the confessor do not end with the peak on the top, but remain open. This is a sign of the supernatural character of what is happening within: the roof remains open toward the sky, because the priest is acting *in persona Christi,* wielding a power given to him from Jesus Himself, and he is administering a Sacrament. This is the "power of the keys," those same crossed keys standing out on the little entrance door of the confessional of Padre Pio. This has nothing to do with the psychoanalyst's couch or the weekly meeting with the personal trainer. Here, in the ancient rite of forgiveness, men reconcile themselves with God.

These old confessionals, essentially identical to the one that Padre Pio of Pietrelcina used, obtained a marvelous synthesis of two aspects apparently incompatible: on one hand, they safeguarded for the penitent and the priest that modesty and privacy which the grate provides to men when they have to stand naked in front of their conscience, revealing exactly the things they are most ashamed of. On the other hand, these confessionals were a "glass show-case window," exhibiting the faithful to the public, which offered the reassuring picture of the absolute normality of confessing one's sins. It sufficed to pass by inside a church to be able to observe the confessional inside, half hidden by a drape, a priest with his head leaning on one side, and glimpse the feet of the penitent crop up from below.

It is difficult to imagine a "promotional message" more efficacious also for the most hardened sinners. Upon seeing that scene, anyone would sooner or later ask himself: if they could do it, why could I not do it, too? You could see, but not hear: you could get only the face of the priest and the wide movements of his hand tracing in the air the sign of the final absolution. Even the unbelievers were seriously touched by that sight, simple and grandiose: throngs of Japanese used to stop, enchanted, in the Dome of Milan to observe distinguished managers dressed in grey suits kneeling down to ask for forgiveness from an old priest dressed in a worn-out cassock.

Afterward, the big box confessionals came into use, perhaps with the chair instead of the kneeler, without a grate between the priest and the penitent, but with closed cabins that impeded the view from outside of the edifying scene of a soul in confession. They are office cubicles for consultations rather than "huts of forgiveness." They are sealed all around, and goodbye to the "open roof" singing praises to the flux of grace coming from above. Not only that: those cubicles are cloistered more and more often in a place set apart from the Church, far from indiscreet glances. In this way, the segregation, the removal of the phenomenon is accomplished: if a Christian does really want confession, he must really look for it. God forbid if anyone coming into a church to see the frescoes of Caravaggio, and, seeing an old fashioned confessional in the isle, were to be suddenly inspired by the desire to repent.

But in consequence of these ambitious schemes, the practical outcome has been a deep crisis of the Sacrament of Confession, which has had its most exemplary peak in certain churches in Holland, where the confessionals have been transformed into storages for cleaning tools.

The advises of Padre Pio

No risks of that kind with the Catholicism of Padre Pio. For this friar with the stigmata, the essence of this extraordinary Sacrament was very clear, beginning with the physical location where the action should take place.

"Padre, what is the confessional?" he was asked once. "It is the throne where God's majesty resides!" The confessional is then the throne of God's divine mercy.

One of his spiritual daughters asked him: "Padre, who are you for us?" The answer, very short, is an extraordinary catechesis on the priesthood: "Among you I am your brother, on the altar a victim, in the confessional a judge." A judge who, obviously, cared about the destiny of every penitent, and who never neglected to help every soul in finding the way to conversion. Padre Pio was very severe with sin, even if he knew well the misery of man and his corrupt nature. From his writings there are found some reflections which even now are very useful in preparing for a good Confession. First:

Never be proud of yourselves because of anything good you may find within you, because every perfect gift comes from above; to God, then, you shall always give honor and glory for it, and you should expect nothing else but the reward of the good you do.

Second:

You shall not be surprised at all by your weaknesses, but, acknowledging yourselves for what you are, you shall blush for your instability and unfaithfulness toward God, and trust in Him, peacefully abandoning yourselves in the arms of the celestial Father, as a tiny child in those of his mother.

Third:

Never shall you exalt yourselves when virtuous, but, receiving all from God, be prompt to give back to him the honor and the glory for it with unceasing thanksgivings.

Fourth:

Do not worry about tomorrow, think about doing good today, and when tomorrow arrives, it will be called today, and then you will think about it.

Clear deals, long friendships

With Padre Pio the deal was clear. For a confession to be valid, all the conditions necessary to this purpose must be fulfilled: a serious and scrupulous examination of conscience, accusation of sins with no intentional omissions, sincere contrition and sorrow for having committed them, just as sincere an intention not to commit them any more by avoiding the occasions of sin, fulfillment of the penance assigned by the priest. Padre Pio had the greatest consideration for the seriousness of these regulations of the Church and used to apply them with simplicity, but also with firmness.

One day a young man stopped in front of him, crying and sobbing with no embarrassment. He asked him: "Why are you crying?" And he replied: "Because you did not give me absolution." Padre Pio consoled him with tenderness, and told him: "Son, you see, I did not deny you the absolution to send you to Hell, but to Paradise."

The decision not to give absolution to the penitent before him caused not a few perplexities for the friar with the stigmata. Some made him realize that it was a very grave responsibility for him because that particular Christian could have died before being able to receive a valid absolution for his sins. In those days in the Church, the firm belief held that the judgment of God could also mean the damnation of souls, and, therefore, to die without being in the grace of God was considered the worst thing that could happen to anyone.

Nowadays, many think that the old fashioned Catholicism, the one that worked profitably for 2,000 years, was a trap for sad men, a torture for the conscience under the unceasing terror of eternal damnation. Feel free to continue to believe in this mystifying deformation of the past. However, the truth is very simple: the souls of those who preceded us lived, it is true, in the holy fear of hell, but they had their sight projected toward the marvelous expectation of Paradise. Padre Pio, referring to the destiny of the people in his care, wrote in one of his letters: "I will stop at the door of Paradise, and I will not enter until all my children will be inside."

Our true Homeland

There was no obsession for sin, then, no sadness with downcast eyes. Simply, the certainty that in life a decisive game, though limited in time, was being played: the one about the eternal destiny of each one of us. Padre Pio writes in his letters:

> Let us have always in front of our eyes the fact that here on earth we are on a battlefield and that in Paradise we will receive the crown. Here is a place of trial and we will receive the reward up there. Here we are in a land of exile and our true homeland is Heaven and to that we have to aspire unceasingly.

At first glance, they seem to be words to be taken for granted, at least for a Catholic. But, at closer look, we notice some epochal differences with respect to a certain theology that triumphed in the 20th century. First: life is a struggle. Second: the battle is fought in view of a reward, and, therefore, Christianity cannot be reduced to the ethics of Kant, which excludes precisely the idea that good must be rewarded. Third: there is a primacy of eternity over time, of the future life over earthly life, and this primacy must warn us about the idea, so widespread today, that the main goal of Catholicism is "human advancement" in this world. "Human advancement" is an undeniable effect of evangelization, as Catholicism is also the source of civilization and progress, but we should not confuse this effect with the main objective of the Church, which is the salvation of the souls entrusted to her.

This is why Padre Pio stayed nailed down for hours and hours in the confessional. He renounced the act of changing the world, instead limiting himself to changing the hearts of the people he met.

In all this work there was a real urgency, expressed by the following words of the saint:

> Who has time, should not waste time; let us not delay until tomorrow what we can do today. The road to Hell is paved with good intentions...[1] After all, who tells us that tomorrow we will be alive?

Orthodoxy and humor

The nice thing is that this Samnite friar, with a character at times rough and with a doctrine firm and uncompromising, and who carried upon him the signs of the Passion and talked about death and damnation without human respect, was at the same time a man full of humor and capable of smiling and making others smile. Whoever imagines the gloom and sadness of the Middle Ages depicted in dark colors by the anti-Catholic black legend, will be left disappointed. With Padre Pio people cried and laughed, just as they did with the rock-solid Catholicism of tradition.

Padre Pio, for example, was not flexible with the penitents who loved to use strange circumlocutions, who, in the end, were beating around the bush. Confession was, for him, in perfect adherence to tradition, something direct and serious, not to be confused with psychological counseling or spiritual direction. In short: make your points few but clear.

One day a certain man showed up in the confessional and began by saying: "Padre, I let myself be tempted by gluttony... " and he went on with a long intricate talk.

Padre Pio cut him short: "Listen, I did not understand a thing you said. Could you tell me clearly what you have done?"

And the man replied: "I have eaten with pleasure..."

---

[1] These are common Italian proverbs.

At this point Padre Pio hit the target and remarked: "What? Would you like to eat with displeasure?"

These were the words of a man who did not underestimate the importance of any discipline, even at the table:

> Never rise from the dinner table without giving due thanks to the Lord. By doing this, we have nothing to fear from wretched gluttony. When eating, watch the excessively sophisticated foods, knowing that little or nothing is needed to satisfy your stomach. Never take more food than needed, and see to it to be temperate in everything, taking care rather to lean toward want than excess. [...] Everything should be regulated by prudence, the rule for all human deeds.

We all are clowns

In summary, Padre Pio was a serious man, and for this very reason he could look at himself and the world with the amused eye of one who nurtures a sane sense of humor. Perhaps because of this human trait, a great many entertainment people, mainly movie and theatre actors, went up to San Giovanni Rotondo to go to confession to him and, in more than one case, to definitively change their way of life.

The comic actor Carlo Campanini was one of these. For this man, his meeting with Padre Pio was decisive to the point that he became one of the friar's spiritual sons. But Campanini was a comic actor, who every evening had to plaster his face with face powder and greasepaint before getting onto stage to play the fool. This aspect of his art often led him to a certain discouragement, because of which he entrusted himself to Padre Pio: How can I become one of your spiritual sons if then every day I have to play the clown to make people laugh? This is what Campanini wondered.

The answer from Padre Pio was a synthesis of his vision of man and of the world: "My son, in this world everybody plays the clown as best he can, in the place where the Lord put him."

The conversation with Carlo Campanini certainly is one of the most well known and surprising incidents of Padre Pio's life. Campanini, born in 1906 in Turin, had made his debut in theatre acting companies, dedicating himself to operetta and comic plays. In the 30s he started a very close-knit comic duo with Erminio Macario. Then, in the 40s, he had an extraordinary success as a movie actor, to the point of acting in up to ten movies per year. The film directors and producers were fighting to have him play the role of the supporting actor, a character naive but good-hearted, clumsy and bizarre. In this role, Campanini acted with the best names of Italian cinema: Totò (*The Two Little Orphans* and *The Rape of the Sabine Women*), Anna Magnani, Carlo Dapporto, Amedeo Nazzari, and Walter Chiari. With the latter he established a working relationship particularly strong both from the human and professional standpoint. The two became very well-known as characters on the TV screen, then in its infancy: even now, many will remember the skit with the famous catch phrase: "Come on, stupid!" Or the *cult* spoof of the notorious "*Sarchiapone*." Campanini was, indeed, a man of success. However, he had a very peculiar trait in his personality: as soon as his commitments allowed, he went to pay a visit to his spiritual father who lived in a small monastery in the mountains of Apulia, and his name was Padre Pio of Pietrelcina.

Carlo Campanini narrates that he ascended to the monastery for the first time to ask the friar, whom he had heard of but whom he did not know, for help in an economic matter. At that time, the comic actor from Turin was not a renowned actor yet, and was always on the road playing in a third-class theatre company together with his wife, leaving their three children with a relative. Not always did the figures add up for the family. That year the acting company arrived in Bari in the spring, and, since the shows were interrupted on Holy Thursday and Good Friday, Carlo thought he would take advantage of this and go up to the friar with the stigmata to ask him to put an end to his vagabond life.

The first meeting held little encouragement: "You people don't let me alone to pray even on these days…What do you want?" Campanini heard these words addressed to him.

"Padre, we are two poor artists…"

"We all are poor…" remarked the sighing Padre Pio. But the confession began. According to what many years later Campanini recounted to journalist Renzo Allegri, things went this way:

> The Padre let me talk. He knew everything about me. He made me promise that I would change my life, and then he gave me the absolution. I did not have the courage to ask him anything, but within myself I kept on repeating: Padre, let me find a job close to my house, even as a warehouse man, as long as I can live near my children."

And, in reality, from that time on Campanini's career took a turn: he was given an important role in the movie *Addio Giovinezza* [*Goodbye Youth*], and the contracts poured in.

A destroyed man

However, if success was by now unstoppable, things were going badly regarding his morals:

> Money and fame had worsened me. I was leading a dissolute life: I had illicit relationships, intricate ones; I was not going to Mass, and I did not want to hear about praying. I felt guilty: that is why I did not want to go back to Padre Pio. I was at the peak of my success, I had custom-built American cars, and the journalists used to write about me saying that I was like "parsley in every soup" because I had a role in all the movies. I lacked nothing. But morally I was destroyed, empty, disillusioned, tired, and dreadfully sad. I envied those who had the courage to take their own life…

It was 1949, and this was the status of the soul of Carlo Campanini: a rich and famous actor who did not feel like living any more. Despite this squalor leading to despair, he found the strength to make a decision which would really change his life: he would go to Padre Pio. But, as Alessandro Pronzato states in his book *Padre Pio Joyful Mystery,* Campanini thought it best to act wisely: he went to confession first in a church in Rome, so that he could spill the beans of his most embarrassing faults on that occasion, thus avoiding the shame of having to recount them to the Friar of Pietrelcina. But Carlo miscalculated badly. In fact, when he showed up to Padre Pio, saying that he had decided to change his way of life and that he had recently gone to confession, he received this answer: "Start from 1946!"

"Father, I went to Confession only a few days ago…"

"I told you to start from 1946," roared Padre Pio, who also called him a coward because he was ashamed to tell his sins, whereas he had had no shame in committing them.

Between Carosello[2] and daily Mass

"That confession," Campanini explains, "changed my life completely. At the end the Padre hugged me and kissed me. He gave me a set of rosary beads as a present, strongly suggesting to use them often, and then he added: 'I will always be near you.'"

From that time on, the actor, who had been a libertine and unhappy with everything, became a serious Catholic, despite the effort needed to keep such commitment: "To keep my promises was not easy, but I held tight." Campanini remained a successful actor, acted in ads shown in *Carosello* which made him even more famous than before (for example, his unforgettable ad for the aperitif Cynar, "against the stress of modern life," in which he was later replaced by Ernesto Calindri). But that very same comic and brilliant actor was going to Mass every day, and as soon as he had some free time, he rushed to San Giovanni Rotondo. He used to go to Mass early in the morning, and pray in church at length. In

---

[2] The first commercials aired on Italian television were all restricted to a 15 minute segment per day called *Carosello* [carousel], where they were all shown in sequence. Each commercial would last 3-5 minutes and some of them were true mini-skits that remained famous in their own right.

the evening he participated in the recitation of the rosary with the friars and the people, and used to kneel at the banister of the choir to be as close as possible to the altar while Padre Pio was giving benediction with the Blessed Sacrament. At the end, all would sing a song to Mary, Mother of God.

One evening the choir started: "I'll go to see Her one day...," followed by the refrain: "In Heaven, In Heaven, In Heaven...," with the melody escalating to high pitches. Carlo Campanini, with his voice half tenor and half baritone, used to stand out above the whole assembly. Meanwhile Padre Pio was listening and singing along. At the third refrain "In Heaven...," the voice of Campanini broke and he was unable to use all the strength needed. Padre Pio looked at him with love. Later in the sacristy he told him: "Hey, Carletto,[3] how hard it is to climb up to Heaven...!" And he: "Padre, if you help me, I will try...!"

Obviously, this new lifestyle did not go unnoticed among the people whom Carlo continued to hang out with. His colleagues made fun of him and called him names: "sanctimonious," "bigoted," "Padre Pio's sacristan," "host eater," "altar server," "devotee," "rosary addict." Nevertheless, he did not get boggled by this, but rather he found the strength to say "no" to those producers and directors who were asking him to act in plays that were now incompatible with his Christian life. Behind the jests and mockeries, however, there was often much envy and personal suffering. So it happened that some of his colleagues indeed went to him as a confidant, at which point Campanini would tell them: "Let us go to Padre Pio. He will help you."

A pair of scoundrels

The truth was that Campanini had found a treasure and he could not avoid talking about it to all his best friends, eager to share it with them. One of these lucky ones was Erminio Macario, another extraordinary Italian comic actor who had linked his suc-

---

[3] "Carletto" (literally, "little Charlie") is an affectionate form of "Carlo."

cess to very successful variety shows featuring attendant dancers and beautiful women more or less undressed. All the biographies of Padre Pio agree in reporting that after a meeting in San Giovanni Rotondo, Macario had a sudden change of life. Macario desired to marry a certain young woman, but he was impeded by a previous marriage. It seems that Padre Pio foretold that he would be able to obtain an annulment from the Sacra Rota, which actually happened in 1951. During their first decisive meeting, Erminio Macario asked the friar if he could continue to act with Campanini or if, for the good of his soul, he should quit. "Of course you can do it, as long as you do not resume certain indecent shows for which you are renowned. If you go on with that line of lewdness, you will never again set foot in this place." Then, addressing both comedians, he added: "Listen now, behave yourselves with a little bit of honor, because, so far, you never did, you scoundrels and nothing else...." Seeing them arrive he would address them: "Look at those faces!" These were benevolent reprimands of a father who was in his heart all happy for that pair of rascals who, at this point, used to get together back-stage to recite the rosary.

Totò, Padre Pio, and a sudden death

Campanini did not stop at Macario, but he brought after him a long line of notorious faces in the world of the performing arts. To meet the friar of the stigmata the following personalities found their way up to San Giovanni Rotondo: Elsa Merlini, Lisa Gastoni, Lea Padovani, Silvana Pampanini, Nino Taranto, Tino Scotti, Carlo Dapporto, and Mario Riva. The meeting with Padre Pio was always a very serious matter, and people knew it. For this reason, also, among the stars of TV, movies, or musicals, things did not always go the right way. This was the case of the great, the very famous Totò.

Carlo Campanini more than once had spoken about the Capuchin friar to Antonio De Curtis,[4] who had manifested a

---

[4] Antonio De Curtis, stage name "Totò," was Italy's most famous comic actor.

serious intention to go see him. But, at the point of doing it, he always found a pretext to delay the appointment. Finally, Totò told Campanini: "Listen, Carletto, I cannot come to Padre Pio. I am not ready yet. I have some desires that I cannot get rid of. When they stop, then I will go to Padre Pio. Agreed?" But Campanini, who then followed Catholic doctrine, certainly could not give his blessing to such reasoning, and he replied immediately in a rather explicit, but efficacious way: "Look, on the radio they said that every day in the world 250,000 people die, and among these, 30% die a sudden death. It is therefore dangerous to your soul to reason as you do." Carlo Campanini says that, at that point, Totò started dancing around the room making the sign of the horns[5] with his fingers. He never again wanted to talk about Padre Pio. Totò died in Rome, during the night of April 15, 1967, of a heart attack. His body was taken to the church of Saint Eligius and received a simple blessing, because his disordered marital status did not allow for the celebration of a funeral. But perhaps not even this time Padre Pio came out defeated. According to Totò's daughter Liliana, the last words of Totò were: "Remember that I am Catholic, Apostolic, and Roman."

A hot potato friar

Another missed convert was Walter Chiari.[6] Campanini, who was as close to him as a brother, says: "He never came to Padre Pio, but he had a deep faith and prayed a lot. He did not want to go to Padre Pio simply because he did not feel worthy." Carlo and Walter left three times for a trip to San Giovanni Rotondo, but, once they arrived in Foggia [about 25 miles from San Giovanni Rotondo], the comedian Chiari would run away saying: "I know that if I come up there I have to change my life and I am not able to do it yet."

---

[5] The horn sign is a symbol that presumably keeps bad luck away, according to a popular superstition.
[6] Walter Chiari was one of Italy's most famous TV stand-up comedians and comic movie actors.

Certainly, this was a mistake. But at least Walter Chiari understood that one could not go to Padre Pio with the attitude of super-
ficiality. Alessandro Pronzato comments:

> Getting close to him was dangerous: you could get burnt
> [...]. When Padre Pio opens the register list book of your duties,
> he becomes merciless. He throws in your face, without much
> consideration, the folder of your faults. If he wishes to put back
> onto the right path one who has gone astray, he certainly does
> not resort to caresses, but he claws him down inexorably, growls
> at him, I would say that he snaps at his ankle, never to let him
> go again. Nor does he even care if he scratches you. He does
> not hesitate to sink his nails into the depth of your conscience
> whenever there is a question of pruning from it the tenacious
> adhesions of evil. If he finds it necessary, he does not think twice
> of resorting to slapping, caring about no one [...]. He uses sand
> paper. His closing speeches leave you without breath: some sort
> of a preview of the final judgment, which sends chills to the
> shrewdest individuals.

We shall settle the score with a difficult God

This is the pedagogy of Padre Pio of Pietrelcina in the confessional, a kind of pedagogy which erases in one shot the image of a
good-natured and even naïve God, with whom it is always possible
to come to a compromise or an agreement. For Padre Pio as a confessor, sin is a serious thing, because it leads the soul to damnation.
"Blasphemy is the surest way to go to Hell." He might have mildly
said that he who blasphemes "breaks his friendship with God" or
that the blasphemers "turn away from the fidelity to the Word."
Instead, he says something extremely down to earth, supplying
a brilliant beam as a satellite navigation system for souls: if you
go in that direction, you will end up in Hell. Amen. A Hell that
obviously exists and is not empty, a Hell which we have to think
about sometimes, if we want to readjust the course of our own life.
The God of Padre Pio is the true God of the true Catholic Faith:
a God not to be taken lightly, who demands to be taken terribly

seriously. A difficult God who transcends man and who, as the French philosopher Jean Guitton explains, establishes a disproportion between Him and His creatures.

Padre Pio and Padre Mandic

Padre Pio's strictness with some sinners stirred perplexities and suggested comparisons with other well-known confessors. Carlo Campanini, who evidently had enough familiarity with the friar to be able to ask him many sorts of questions, one day challenged him by saying: "Padre, I heard that Padre Leopoldo Mandic, a saintly Capuchin who lives in Padova, gives confessions 18 hours a day and never sends away anyone without absolution…"

In fact, the fame of St. Leopoldo Mandic was at that time enormous: he was a little friar to whom very many penitents were going. As for his personal features one would be stricken by his short height, which did not prevent him from becoming a true giant of Confession. Going to confession to Padre Leopoldo was a brief thing, very brief. He never elaborated with words, explanations, conversations. He had learned from the catechism of St. Pius X that brevity characterizes a good confession. In a letter to a priest, Padre Leopoldo writes:

> Forgive me, Father, forgive me if I dare…you see, we in the confessional, do not have to show off our culture; we do not have to speak about things beyond the capability of each soul, nor do we have to digress with explanations; otherwise, with our imprudence, we spoil what the Lord is accomplishing in them. It is God, and only God, who operates in the souls! We have to disappear, limit ourselves in helping out this divine intervention in the mysterious ways of their salvation and sanctification.

After all, it is not even certain that St. Leopoldo Mandic had a style with penitents that differed from that of his confrere of Pietrelcina, because some biographers describe him, too, as: "belligerent and capable of firing up in harsh and unexpected bursts, like his compatriot St. Jerome." In fact, like St. Jerome, he asked God for the gift of self-control: "Have pity of me, for I am Dalmatian!" On the other hand, his fame for sanctity was considerable. All the people in Padua knew him for his goodness: "Padre Leopoldo, O may he be blessed! That one for sure is good!"[7] Elsewhere Padre Leopoldo also writes: "They tell me that I am too good, but, if someone comes up and kneels before me, is this not a sufficient proof that he begs God for forgiveness?"

Padre Mandic in fact met Padre Pio when, during the Great War, he was forced to move to Southern Italy because of his Hapsburg nationality.

The truth of the matter is that Padre Pio, faced with the criticism of Companini, his spiritual son, certainly did not remain silent: "What do you think, that I know nothing about it? Of course I know it. But remember that He sends to me His most obstinate sinners, and I have to deal with them..." But Campanini did not give up: "Nonetheless, you, as spiritual father, take upon yourself a big responsibility in sending away a sinner with no absolution. Think about it: what if he, soon after exiting the church, gets hit by a stroke and dies?"

"In case I were wrong" answers Padre Pio "do you think that He will be wrong too? Be at peace, my son, He will put things right..."

Besieged by celebrities

It seems a paradox. The more severely the saint with the stigmata treated sinners, the more they flocked to him. His confessional was like a constant destination for pilgrimages, and among hundreds of thousands of anonymous faces, quite often it was possible to see some personalities who were used to having their faces on the front pages of well-known magazines or newspapers. They were the VIPs of the beautiful society, or politicians, singers, and sports champions who were there, a few inches away from a Capuchin speaking in slang, and they became, nonetheless, equal

---

[7] These words of an implied resident of Padua are written in the local dialect in the original text, which is impossible to render with an English equivalent.

to all the other men on earth. This is indeed the "democracy" of Catholicism: even a Very Important Person is, after all, a sinner, a son of Adam, and in need of the salvation of Christ. Obviously, he will be saved if, and only if, he wants to be saved. And so it was that, in San Giovanni Rotondo, there lined up Aldo Fabrizi, Tino Scotti, Lucia Bosè, Maria Josè of Savoy,[8] Tazio Nuvolari,[9] the sculptor Francesco Messina, Gino Latilla, Carla Boni, Beniamino Gigli,[10] the Empress Zita of Austria and her children, Albert of Liege,[11] Cardinal Giuseppe Siri, Helenio Herrera[12] with all the players of his great team *Inter* (the friar predicted they would win the championship), Gino Bartali, who took along his friend and lifelong opponent: Fausto Coppi.[13] These are the names of just a few.

A lone man in the lead

Coppi had gone to San Giovanni Rotondo with his wife. When Padre Pio saw him, he asked him: "Where is Mrs. Coppi?" When the woman came up to him he said to her: "Mrs. Coppi, watch that he does not put you under!"[14] Everybody started laughing, obvi-

---

[8] A member of Italy's royal family, Maria Josè of Savoy was Italy's last queen just prior to the referendum in 1946 that abolished the monarchy.

[9] Nuvolari was a legendary race car driver from the 1930s through the early 1950s.

[10] Gigli was an internationally known opera tenor who died in 1957.

[11] Prince Albert of Liege eventually became king of Belgium.

[12] Herrera was the Argentinian-born coach of the *Inter* soccer team of Milan, which dominated Italian soccer for a good part of the 60s. He was the first soccer coach to break the million dollar yearly salary, which began an avalanche of mega-contracts for coaches and players alike, as well as the globalization of the market for coaches and players alike.

[13] Bartali and Coppi were lifelong rivals in bicycle racing from the 1930s to the 1950s. Bartali, nicknamed "the Pious" because of his religiosity, won three Tour of Italy and two Tour de France competitions, and Coppi, commonly referred to as "the Super Champion," won five Tour of Italy and two Tour de France competitions. All of the others mentioned but not specifically identified in the text were singers and actors popular in Italy in the 40s, 50s, and 60s.

[14] The Italian text reads "*Signora Coppi, attenta che non t'accoppi.*" and is a play on words: "*Coppi*" is akin to "*coppa*," which means in this case "tombstone," and "*accoppi*" literally means "kill, do away with, dispose of."

ously thinking of a joke, a pun. Seven days later, Fausto Coppi left his wife to move in with an actress, the so-called "lady in white."[15]

But Padre Pio, being a good Catholic priest, loved sinners and unceasingly prayed for their conversion. He did so also for "the Super Champion," to whom he used to have delivered occasional messages and also some reproaches: "Tell Fausto that if he does not go back to his family, the hand of the Lord will fall heavily upon him."

The biographers of Coppi report that, after all, Fausto was not at all indifferent to the reprimands he was getting from the Church. According to Enrico Bassano, a reporter who was his good friend: He wanted to go back to his wife and was waiting for the right time to put order in his life. Then, suddenly, he got a mysterious "Asian" fever, and was rushed to the emergency room of the hospital in Tortona at 5:30 pm on New Year's Day in 1960. Coppi died in room number 4 on the morning of January 2, 1960. During the night though, he had seen again for the last time his wife Bruna and his daughter Marina.

To convert, or the conjugation of the verb: "to become a Catholic"

Padre Pio often had his penitents recite the following prayer: "I entrust my past, O Lord, to Your mercy, my present to Your love, my future to Your providence." It would be well for everyone to recite this formula often, so true and so rich of hope for every soul, even the farthest from God, even the one most enslaved by sin. After all, Padre Pio has been the living proof that Jesus Christ, He who "*pertransit benefaciendo*," "passed by doing good," today also wants to reach every heart and draw it to Himself. No "prey" is out of the reach of Christ.

But, what does it mean "to be converted"? Katharina Tangari, who knew Padre Pio well, writes:

---

[15] Giulia Occhini

Conversion is the happy transformation in Christ through which we receive the joy of faith, the fervor for the commandments, and the love for the Sacraments. With this, a new life starts for us, the life of salvation, which those fervent for Christ so keenly desire for all men. Padre Pio showed to countless souls this way for salvation.

There never was a class of people who escaped the work of persuasion and consolation of the Friar of Pietrelcina. There are memorable cases of the conversion of men holding important roles in the freemasonic lodges. One of these was Alberto Del Fante, who summarizes his story as follows:

> I was a freemason; I was an atheist; I believed in nothing. Padre Pio gave me life from every point of view. Today I pray, I go to Mass every Sunday, I am pleased when my children, before meals, make the sign of the Cross to thank God who gives us our daily bread. Now, I receive Communion and I am happy when God comes into my body. Whoever will have my courage, will have my happiness.

Courage, this was what was needed for men of hardened conscience after years of absence from the Church, and perhaps even of enmity toward that Christ Whom the poet Giosuè Carducci[16] so addressed in his *Odi Barbare*: "*Cruciato martire tu cruci gli uomini, / tu di tristizia l'aer contamini*" ["Crucified martyr, you crucify men, / you contaminate the air with sadness"]. For the enemies of the Church, Jesus contaminates the air with sadness, but those same adversaries discover with surprise, when taken by grace, that in Him there is only joy.

The lawyer Cesare Festa was also a big shot in freemasonry. In his biography dedicated to Padre Pio, Rino Camilleri writes of Festa:

---

[16] Giosuè Carducci was an Italian poet of the late 1800s who won the Nobel Prize for Literature in 1906.

He was the head of the masonic tribunal in Liguria [Northwestern Italian region]. One meeting changed his life. Padre Pio saw him in San Giovanni Rotondo, approached him and asked if by any chance he was a freemason. He, rather astonished, answered affirmatively, and that his job in the lodges was the one to make life difficult for the Church. Padre Pio grabbed his hands and took him aside. He recounted to him the parable of the prodigal son. Then he gave him Confession. The conversion of the lawyer Festa was not appreciated by his freemason "brothers," who put him on trial and expelled him (although in reality Festa had left on his own). On the morning of the masonic trial, Cesare Festa could smell the unmistakable, very strong fragrance indicating the presence of Padre Pio, who, smiling, used to define this phenomenon as "candies for children." When Festa set out on a pilgrimage to Lourdes, the newspaper *Avanti!*[17] whipped him with sarcasm: "A freemason goes to Lourdes." Upon his return, Cesare Festa became a Franciscan tertiary.

With Padre Pio, half-measures and compromises worthy of small time street-smart cheats could not work. This was true regarding the moral life and, even more, in the field of doctrine and of dogmatic theology. When facing Christians of other persuasions, such as Orthodox or Protestants, the friar did not limit himself by suggesting a generic "ecumenical embrace"; he did not emphasize "the points in common"; nor did he exhort to "remain with coherence each in his own church." The saint instead put before the souls the usual radical choices: either on this side or on the other, making them understand that, also for the salvation of their souls, there was really a big difference.

Mrs. Rina Caterinovich d'Ergiu, who belonged to the Greek Orthodox Church, went to Padre Pio in the beginning of October 1923. She started a spiritual journey to become a Catholic, which eventually took place in the spring of the following year. On that

---

[17] *Avanti! [Forward!]* is the daily newspaper of the Italian Socialist Party. Ironically, Fascist dictator Benito Mussolini had been its editor in the early part of the 20th century.

occasion she brought with her an old aunt who, speaking to the friar, explained that she did not wish to convert because she felt that her religion, Greek Orthodox, was very close to the Catholic one; that she was now too old to change religions; and that she would cause too much pain to her relatives if she did so. The answer of Padre Pio summarizes harshly the doctrine of the Capuchin: "Do you believe that before the Lord your relatives will answer for you?" The woman said: "Thank you for your kindness, and forgive me if I displeased you." And Padre Pio: "Not displeasure, you gave me a real anguish!" Sometime later, in Capri, the woman renounced her religion and became a Catholic.

CHAPTER 4

The Little Flowers[1]
Of San Giovanni Rotondo

Padre Pio is the agent of extraordinary miracles,
but he confides with sincere humility to be only
a poor friar who prays and celebrates Mass

Bilocation, scents and extraordinary aromas, the ability to "see" the thoughts of people, knowledge of the most diverse languages without having ever studied them, descents into Hell, visits to Purgatory, healings, prophecies, and conversions: Padre Pio's case is one of a kind, the case of a man who had experienced an unusual abundance of phenomena definitely inexplicable, at least according to the categories of science and of the physical world. What usually is considered the extraordinary, paradoxically, becomes the ordinary in his life. The innumerable biographies about him contain testimonies of phenomena disclosed by those who met him, including skeptics above suspicion, leading to the realization that the human story of Francesco Forgione escapes any comparison, and is impossible to relate to any equivalent: Padre Pio is Padre Pio, and that's it.

A living scandal

From one standpoint, Padre Pio is a scandal. He is a scandal outside, but also within the Catholic world. He cannot be understood by the usual followers of scientism, hopeless and close-

---

[1] The title here recalls the famous book *The Little Flowers of Saint Francis*, written by an anonymous medieval author and recounting the life of Saint Francis.

minded, who try to circumscribe the world inside a test-tube or in a chemical formula. Neither can he be understood by the arrogant and prejudiced theologians, who wish to narrow down Christianity to the reading of the Word and to biblical exegesis. Both pay the consequences of an erroneous position. To understand Padre Pio one must bend the knee, and bend his own untamed pride as well. This is a lesson to be learned precisely from this Samnite friar, who never became exalted by the extraordinary gifts he had received, which were the real motives for people coming to San Giovanni Rotondo from all over the world.

It is obvious that never so many pilgrims would have crowded around the friar with the stigmata if he did not represent some sort of an open door between earth and Heaven, a meeting point between the finite and the infinite, between time and eternity. If he had given magnificent speeches, or if he had explained the true meaning of an Aramaic verb, he would have secured the public applause in some convention of scholars, or he might have merited the front page of an influential newspaper. Instead, Padre Pio has been, more simply, an instrument of grace. For this reason, the least ones and the sinners, the common people and uneducated folks, the careless and unrepentant protagonists of the world of show business, and some freemasons with an unsatisfied heart have very often understood him, and sought never to leave him again.

All of them had been conquered by the disarming normality of a character that was completely abnormal. This man, who could be seen in two different places at the same time, or who unveiled to penitents which sins they should accuse themselves of even before they had opened their mouth, was an impressive champion of humility. He would say about himself:

> I am not at all good. I really do not know how this habit of St. Francis that so unworthily I wear, does not run away from me...The least of the scoundrels on earth, if compared to me, is made of gold.

At the 60th anniversary of taking his religious habit, while the faithful and his confreres congratulated him profusely, Padre Pio broke down in uncontrollable weeping and, covering his face, said: "Sixty years of unworthiness." Other times, after having spent his days in the confessional, the friar had said that he felt like a "volcano of scum."

This extraordinary sensitivity regarding one's own limitations and weaknesses is a typical symptom of sanctity: it is the fruit of a soul living in the light, and captures clearly what a hardened heart and a toughened conscience do not see. Thus, George Bernanos is right when he writes that in the world there exist only two categories of people: "the sinners, who think they are righteous, and the righteous, who think they are sinners." That is why, for instance, a saintly king like Baldwin of Belgium, a sovereign who preferred to risk losing his throne rather than signing the law to legalize abortion, could pray like this: "Oh my God, forgive the insect that I am, make me humble and happy to have been created a little thing."

In his letters, Padre Pio often returns to the theme of the vice of vainglory to warn himself and his interlocutors about the terrible lure which inflames in the heart of all men:

> This vice must be pushed away so much more as it has no opposing virtue to fight it. In fact, every vice has its remedy and its contrasting virtue: anger is knocked out by meekness, envy by charity, pride by humility, and so on; only vainglory has no opposite virtue to be fought with. It sneaks into the most holy actions; and even into humility itself; if you are not careful, it proudly puts up its tent.

Recalling an image used by St. Jerome, Padre Pio compares vainglory to a shadow:

> The shadow follows the body everywhere; it even measures its steps. The body runs, and vainglory runs with it; if the body walks slowly, it follows suit; the body sits down, and it assumes the same posture.

In this matter the Capuchin Saint showed a natural practicality, as he always did, in every matter throughout his life: as a priest he did not restrict himself to warning about a danger for the salvation of souls, he also clearly and precisely indicated the necessary means to do good and avoid evil. Do you want to be humble? Then, Padre Pio says:

Think of yourself as you really are: a nullity, a misery, a weakness, a source of perversity with no limits nor mitigating circumstances, capable of changing good into bad, of arrogating the good and excusing yourselves when you do evil, and, for love of the same evil, you are able to despise the Highest Good.

Are you oppressed by tribulations, are you unjustly criticized, are you not kept in due esteem by your colleagues? Here is Padre Pio's medicine:

Never complain about offenses, wherever they come from, remembering that Jesus, our exemplary role model, was saturated with ignominy by men's iniquity, without ever uttering a lament.

Resentment makes you restless, and rancor harbors in the depth of your soul, ready to fire up in a blaze of revenge?

You shall excuse all with Christian charity, keeping in mind the example of the Divine Master, who excused even His executioners before His Father.

This advice strikes us even harder when we consider it comes from a friar full of ailments and pains and living 81 years in a veritable Calvary, full of suspicions and misunderstandings; of mysterious illnesses and calumnies; and surrounded by noisy and intrusive pilgrims, by penitents in the confessional loaded with sins, and by reporters and meddlers wanting to see "the sensation."

A life full of strange events

Some episodes from the infancy of Francesco Forgione seem premonitory, almost forerunners of the wonders that will make this friar an inexplicable phenomenon to entire teams of doctors and scholars. Obviously, all of this must be considered within the context of a fully normal Italian story, where the extraordinary remains mostly hidden, like an underground river, under the ordinariness of daily life.

Francesco was the fourth of eight children, three of whom died at a very tender age. He was born in a corner of the Kingdom of Italy, a very young nation taking its very first steps in opposition to the Catholic Church, even though its population was 99% Catholic. The child who will later become Padre Pio was born on May 25, 1887. In that same year Francesco Crispi, leading figure of freemasonry, had the crucifixes removed from the schools of the realm. But in Pietrelcina, at that time a small municipality in the area of Samnium, a mountainous land between the regions of Campania and Molise, everyone was Catholic and devoted to the Blessed Mother. Padre Pio's father, Zi' Grazio,[2] was named after Our Lady of All Graces, Patroness of Pietrelcina.

The Forgione house was similar to millions of other Italian houses at that time: three small rooms, a ceiling made of reeds, very small door and windows, probably also because of an absurd tax on windows conceived by the voracious internal revenue office of the realm. Francesco's story reads like other ordinary Italian stories: his father, Grazio, is 26 and his mother, Giuseppina di Nunzio, is 28. His family was like many others: not rich nor poor, happy to have what was needed, but needing to deal with financial straits, such that the father of the family was compelled, as were many of his countrymen at that time, to go overseas to make a living.

---

[2] Vernacular meaning literally "uncle Grace," where the proper name is understood to mean the supernatural gift of God, not the human quality. It is common in small Italian villages to refer even to people not related by blood as "uncle" or "aunt" if sufficient familiarity exists between them.

In this absolutely ordinary scene, little Francesco burst in, for soon he brought in a bit of disarray. First of all, because of his name, chosen by his parents not in honor of the Little Poor Man of Assisi, but of St. Francis of Paola.

The life of this saint from Calabria,[3] who was born in 1416, and died at the age of 91 at the court of the King of France, is somewhat analogous to that of Padre Pio, including some extraordinary prodigies. St. Francis of Paola had a majestic bearing, a long beard and disheveled hair. He lived and fostered a spirit of prayer and mortification, and, despite the hermit life he had chosen, he was often besieged by people of every social rank who went to him for counsel. People knew about his extraordinary ability to extinguish fire, as he was capable of handling burning embers and coals with no harm to himself.

But, beyond these phenomena of historic nature, some mysterious aspects manifested themselves in the life of the little Francesco Forgione. As a newborn, he cried unremittingly, to the point that his father, exasperated by the sleepless nights after very hard day's work in the fields, one day pretended to throw away the unbearably whining bundle. All sources say that, from that time on, the baby stopped making a fuss. Years later, according to what Rino Camilleri reports, Padre Pio explained the occurrence: "When they switched off the light, hordes of monsters drew near him, and he cried. When the light was on, they disappeared. Grazio, of course, could not know anything about it."

The child who was praying in the midst of sorrow

Also the character of the child is peculiar from the start. On one hand, Francesco does not seem to be abnormal, does not seem unstable, or a pathologic case. One of his old friends, many years later, said: "He was a boy like all of us." Also in his young age he had some tantrums, some scuffles with his older brother Michele,

---

[3] South-western region of Italy facing Sicily.

some pranks in the style of *Marcellino, Pane e Vino*.[4] But, on the other hand, his behavior reveals an intense spiritual life, deep and unusual, from childhood. According to some biographers, when they sent him to herd the sheep, they often found him absorbed in prayer or in building nativity scenes with mud. With other shepherd boys he played the "game of the procession," while the unattended sheep wandered astray to graze within the crops, to the anger of the farmers.

Francesco was an obedient and taciturn child, so that some of his peers used to call him in dialect "the deaf wolf," an epithet given to people of a taciturn and very reserved nature. His mother used to exhort him to go out and play a little with his friends, but he would refuse: "I don't want to go because they curse."

In 1896, his father took him along with him to Altavilla Irpina for the feast of St. Peregrine. On that occasion there was a big fair, and Zi' Grazio wanted to buy a horse. Francesco was nine years old and spent the night sleepless in anticipation of the big day. In the morning, after a few hours' journey on the back of a donkey, father and son arrived at the shrine already overflowing with faithful. People were numerous, and they manifested their faith in a simple and obviously showy way. At a certain point a man muscled in through the crowd, carrying in his arms a child gravely malformed. Everyone was struck dumb. When he reached the icon of the saint in the church, he began his heartrending prayer. Zi' Grazio wanted to leave the church, but Francesco insisted on staying to pray a little more. In the meantime, the father of the poor creature had put down, rather, had literally thrown down his child onto the altar, telling St. Peregrine: "*O pigliatillo o dammillo buono*" [dialect for "Either you take him back, or you give him back to me healthy"]. After rolling on the ground, the child sat down, sane and normal, among the shouts and excitement of the bystanders.

This episode has been easily interpreted by some biographers as the first miracle of Padre Pio. Nevertheless one thing is sure: during

---

[4] *Marcellino, Bread and Wine*, is the title of a movie about a young boy who was bringing bread and wine to the Crucified Christ.

those minutes full of pathos, the young Forgione experienced very closely the suffering of men, in particular that of a father for the sickness of his own son, and he touched firsthand the request for salvation that the creatures direct to God through the saints. That scene was nothing but the repetition of hundreds, thousands of incessant requests that Jesus of Nazareth heard every day addressed to Him while passing through the roads of Galilee and Judea. At the same time, little Francesco could witness with his own eyes the irresistible power of prayer, specifically of his own prayer. The episode occurring in the shrine of St. Peregrine represents at least a foreshadowing of the kind of future reserved for the young Forgione: a life of sufferings and of supernatural answers to all of the sea of sorrow.

A vocation with the beard

When it is said that, to understand Padre Pio, one must bend his knees, the intention is to point to an actual method. In fact, one must take on the viewpoint of faith, to allow his reason to "bear" the events that accompany the story of the most famous Capuchin in the world. The chronicles say that Francesco made his decision to consecrate his life to God when he was five, in front of the altar. This news item is already *per se* astounding, if compared with a certain way of thinking of our times, according to which the ideal faith is the "adult" one, the educated one, one of the intellectual faith, and therefore, it is absolutely out of reach for a five-year-old child. In a time like ours it is shocking that a child can speak of consecrating himself to God: ours is a time when the mere idea of the existence of "minor seminaries," those established for boys in junior high, is abhorred by almost all of the dioceses, which, in a few decades, have turned the vocation to the priesthood into an option for former bank employees in their thirties and unfulfilled in their life.

At the time of the young Francesco Forgione, it was much more normal for the children to think that, as adults, they might like to become priests, or nuns. After all, in Pietrelcina, the little village of Francesco, one could witness every Sunday afternoon an eloquent scene. When the church bell rang at the hour of 4 pm, a strange procession began to wind through the streets. Ahead of everybody, a boy carried the cross and behind him came the sacristan, ringing a jingle bell: it was the call for catechism. At that point, boys and girls of various ages came out of the front doors of their homes and followed the parade. Obviously, there were also ones reluctant to partake in this kind of "Catholic draft," and Michele Forgione was one of these. In those cases the mothers were the ones who pushed forth the more rebellious children out of the door. These methods of persuasion were completely unnecessary for Francesco, who was more than willing to go to catechism class. As they passed from street to street, along the way, the line swelled, until they arrived at the village church, where the pastor was waiting to educate these little souls.

The phenomenon of Padre Pio is certainly unique and unrepeatable, and cannot be explained only in human terms. But we must realize that grace and the supernatural are always infused into the human and into nature. Behind a Padre Pio there are Jesus and Mary, the Trinity, and the saints. But also a Catholic father and mother, a pastor ready to teach the fundamentals of Christian doctrine, and a community where normal people on Sunday do not go to the shopping mall but to Mass and to "doctrine" [catechism].

On the other hand, it was not at all commonplace in those civilized and Christian days that the vocational choice of a child should be "blessed" by the apparition of Jesus in person, a fact confirmed by the testimony of Padre Benedetto of San Marco in Lamis, spiritual director of Padre Pio in the novitiate. Francesco Forgione had his feet well planted on the ground: he was a man, not an angel or a ghost. But he lived constantly in the presence of that invisible but totally real world that common people either ignore, or believe in by an act of faith.

One day, Padre Agostino of San Marco in Lamis, who was at that time his confessor, heard the young Friar Francesco Forgione ask him the following surprising question: "Why, you mean that you do not see Our Lady?" This meant that our man thought it was common, for a religious, to see the Mother of God. This is only a small opening into the mysterious and ineffable dimension which only the great mystics can experience and, with much effort, try to describe to the common people.

But, with Padre Pio surprises never end. If on one hand he had this absolutely vertical projection, this direct line with the supernatural, on the other hand he was also supremely human. For instance, he had made up his mind that the religious order of his choice should be only one that allowed its friars to have a long beard. Young Francesco had been fascinated by Friar Camillo of Sant'Elia a Pianisi, a Capuchin in the convent of Morcone who occasionally came to Pietrelcina to collect alms. According to the description of Rino Camilleri in his book *Life of Padre Pio*, this friar was "tall, grave, with a long black beard [...] a solemn figure who talked with a gentle and charming voice."

Francesco, probably, saw in this Fra Camillo a role model and, when he manifested his intention to become a friar, he said that he absolutely had to be a bearded friar. His father did not oppose his vocation but rather, not without sacrifices, did all he could to allow his child to study and prove whether he had the necessary intellectual qualities to undertake such a demanding call. Francesco did not stand out with his grades, but put much effort into studying, spending days and days at the books, and answering to his friends who came to ask him to go out and play: "Later, later... "

Then, after attaining a more than acceptable preparation, he had to try to enter the seminary of the Capuchins in Morcone. However, the Provincial Father explained that at that time they had no room in the seminary. Then, his uncle Pellegrino tried to convince Francesco to pursue his vocation in another congregation: let the Capuchins go, but try with the Franciscans in Benevento, or the Redemptorists in Sant'Angelo a Cupolo. But Francesco was unmovable: if they don't grow their beards, that was it. This peculiar obstinacy drove Francesco into the order of the Capuchins, which laid the foundations for all the events that followed.

Si non satis, memento paupertatis

On January 6, 1903, the young man ceased to be Francesco Forgione and entered the novitiate in the seminary of Morcone to become Fra Pio. He was welcomed into the monastery by a door-keeper friar whom he knew very well: that certain Fra Camillo with the very beautiful beard who had impressed him so much as a begging friar. On the morning of January 7, the novice awoke in the little cell assigned to him, cell number 18. The water in the pitcher, set next to a rudimentary washbowl, had become a block of ice.

The icy water in the freezing cell indicates the status of the living conditions in the Capuchin Novitiate in 1903. (Also in that year, by the way, Pope Pius X was elevated to the head of the Church after the death of Leo XIII.) The time spent in the novitiate was used for a serious discernment about the vocation of the aspiring Capuchin postulants. The means to accomplish this verification were strictness and austerity. The novices were encouraged to practice sacrifices and self-denial. After all, the rules were clear, starting, for example, with the poster standing high in the monastery of Morcone: "Either penance, or Hell."

As we read the details of that community life freely embraced by men exactly like us in physical and mental makeup, we readily realize that the thriving spiritually produced in this type of austerity, is, in its own way, a miracle, too. Of course, living conditions of even the lay people at that time were not as easy and comfortable as those offered by the "world" of our day. Granted also, that in those days the inclination toward sacrifice and hardship was much more developed than the feeble acts we are able to demonstrate in our present time. But, even after considering this chronological-cultural recalibration, even after putting everything into its proper context and in its historical perspective, we still remain in awe upon observing what was demanded from a young man in order for him to gain entrance into the much desired life as a Capuchin. He was sleeping on a bed made out of four planks placed across two shaky trivets. The mattress, yes, there was a mattress, consisted of a sack filled as well as it could be with dry corn leaves. The washbowl with the pitcher and a rudimentary table completed the simple furnishings in the room. Written on the main beam of the small room an eloquent phrase stood out: "Too much talking will not last without sin."

The novices slept bundled in their habit, and they took care not to wrinkle it by keeping their hands crossed over their chests. The clothes were very rough and always either too tight or too loose. A heater did not exist, and food was scarce, but one must not complain about it, because, as summarized on a notice that stood out in the refectory: "*Si non satis, memento paupertatis,*" "If you do not have enough, remember poverty."

The rhythm of the hours of the day was kept by prayer and penance: at midnight the young men arose to go to the choir to recite Matins and Lauds. Then, at 5 o'clock in the morning, all must again arise. The call for the friars was not the melodic sound of a jingle bell, but a series of harsh blows knocked against a small wooden board, the "*battola.*" The novices had to keep their eyes to the ground and their mouths closed. There were about 150 days of fasting throughout the year. They could not amuse themselves with books other than the *Constitutions* of the Order and the *Rules.* They were allowed to read up to 15 pages, and when finished they read the same pages all over again.

Someone did not want that young man to become a friar

Bilocations and inexplicable healings, fights with the demon, and stigmata are very exceptional phenomena, no doubt about it. But also this kind of life, embraced for love of Christ, and this relentless daily divesting of the old man to make room for the Lord are somewhat miraculous. Especially if we look at them through our eyes of secularized and earth-bound men, concerned with conquering a little piece of ephemeral paradise here on earth, hanging onto our life which inexorably ends, and with an insensitivity to the real one, the eternal life to come.

To all the privations and sacrifices required of all novices, we have to remember the additional load of sufferings and pains that Padre Pio himself had to endure alone. Many witnesses remember, for instance, that this friar had the "gift of tears": he used to cry at the passion of Christ. He kept by his knees a handkerchief with which he tried to hide the swelling in his eyes which formed in those moments of total, intense participation in the sacrifice of Christ.

Then there was the devil, who never really left him alone. For everyone, including Padre Pio, there were the usual temptations which trouble every normal human being: envy, anger, gossip, impure thoughts, sloth, and so on. For the youth of Pietrelcina, the problem was magnified by terrifying visions, physical struggles with the devils, and ailments of every kind. Once he heard noises coming from the cell adjacent to his. He knew that it had been empty for long time and decided to take a look through the small window to see what was going on. An enormous black dog suddenly jumped out of it and landed on the roof of the opposite building, after making an impossible leap. One can imagine the young friar's fright.

There were also the troubles caused by his body. The condition of his health had always been poor, to the point that, as a Capuchin, he left the monastery many times, spending long periods of convalescence in his Pietrelcina. Every time he went back to his mission, his health declined dramatically: it seemed as if somebody did not want that young man to be a friar. The plan indeed was almost on the verge of succeeding, because his Superiors became fed up with his going back and forth, with that wandering about among the various monasteries in the hope of finding one where he could feel a little better, where those mysterious massive fevers would abate, fevers whose temperatures reached 48° C [118° F], so that a special wide-range thermometer had to be used to measure them.

At the end, San Giovanni Rotondo was chosen just as a place for the possible convalescence of the young friar: a quiet and secluded place, on a mountain, where he could stay a few months to recover. Padre Pio arrived there on March 18, 1918, and never left.

Non est abbreviata manus Domini

Padre Pio remained always in San Giovanni Rotondo. But very many witnesses have sworn they saw him and talked to him in other places in Italy and in the world. Technically, this phenomenon is called bilocation, a special state that allows a person to be simultaneously in two separate places. If a miracle can be defined as the momentary suspension of a law of physics or of nature, bilocation is a fully perfect example. And Padre Pio was the agent of this extraordinary phenomenon innumerable times, to the point that it is difficult, if not impossible, to reconstruct exactly all of the episodes.

It is easy to imagine the skepticism, even the ridicule that follows a description of an episode of bilocation. Incredulity is understandable from those who deny God and reduce man to a matter of flesh and bone that originates from nothing and destined for nothing. An atheist cannot understand bilocation, because in his limited horizon there is no God. Padre Pio met many characters of this kind, and he was able to lead the way of conversion for many of them. Perhaps he used precisely the weapon of bilocation. The friar with the stigmata had a profound compassion for unbelievers, although at the same time he did not justify them from a rational stand point. He loved them but he could not understand them, as he used those sane categories of Scholastic thought brought to the highest splendor by St. Thomas Aquinas and solemnly elevated to dogma by the First Vatican Council, which established to be an undeniable truth of Catholic doctrine the possibility to know with the use of reason the existence of God. Padre Pio used to say, with remarks that remind us of the great English convert G. K. Chesterton:

> I feel so much pity for the atheists. How can they be so in a world where the grass grows, where the sun shines, where the birds sing, really I cannot understand. They are people lacking imagination.

While it is understandable that an unbeliever would eschew bilocation, it is not understandable that a Catholic would be incredulous, prejudiced, or even hostile to the accounts of bilocation in the life of Padre Pio. Given that God exists, that He is the God who revealed Himself through the embodiment of Jesus Christ, and that we know Him in the Christ, why should He not allow to occur other phenomena of this magnitude? Should He limit His omnipotence to the dimensions perceptible and comprehensible only by our small intelligence? Should He conform to the standards and fashions of our times? Josemaria Escrivà, the founder of *Opus Dei*, who shared with Padre Pio the abhorrence for the "new Mass" and kept on celebrating the one of all times, very clearly explains the weakness of this obtuseness of some believers: "God is immutable" writes Escrivà (No. 586 of *The Way*). He continues:

> We need men of faith: and the prodigies we read about in Sacred Scripture will happen again. *Ecce non est abbreviata manus Domini*—Behold, the hand of the Lord is not shortened!

The same Josemaria explains:

> I am not one who seeks miracles. I already told you that to hold strong to my faith the miracles in the Holy Gospel are more than enough for me. But I pity those Christians—even pious ones, even "apostolic" ones—who smile when they hear talk of extraordinary means, of supernatural events. I feel like telling them: "Yes, even now there are miracles; we ourselves would perform them if we had faith!"

The long list of prodigies

Evidently, Padre Pio of Pietrelcina had a robust kind of faith, and thus, he became an instrument of the wonderful intervention of God. The list of prodigious events linked to the friar with the stigmata is endless. Rino Camilleri, in his biography of the saint, refers to some particularly impressive ones.

A mother of five was dying of double pneumonia and went into an irreversible coma. At that point, her husband and children stood around Padre Pio to invoke the grace. "I could not take it anymore," said the friar in person, "when those sobbing children were pulling me from all sides and that poor man had neither more voice nor tears to express his distress. Then I said to St. Joseph: 'No, this is not possible, you cannot let them suffer like this... Take her case and heal her, St. Joseph, for the love of God...'" Padre Pio told her husband that she would revive on Easter. Sure enough, punctually, just when the Easter bells started ringing and the priest started singing the *Gloria*, the woman got off her bed completely healed.

The cases of the saint's bilocation are innumerable and all supported by testimonies, sometimes given by very important persons. Among those in show business, for example, not a few of them have reported that they had such a prodigious meeting with the friar: among others who have spoken about it are the actor Carlo Campanini, the singer Gino Latilla, and the singer-songwriter Lucio Dalla. While he was tranquilly living in the small monastery of San Giovanni Rotondo, Padre Pio was at the same time in the United States saving, by holding him in his arms, a child fallen from the 53rd floor of a skyscraper. Or he was in Africa, freeing a nun from prison. Dom Orione, who was always a great defender of Padre Pio, saw him show up in St. Peter's Square on the day of the beatification of St. Therese of Lisieux. Needless to say, that on those occasions the friar had never left his monastery.

"I entrust this creature to you. She is a precious stone"

One of the most sensational cases occurred on January 18, 1905. It took place in Udine,[5] in a stately mansion in Deciani Street, at the corner of Divisione Julia Street. Giovanni Battista Rizzani was in bed, dying. His wife Leonilde Serrao attended him, despite the fact that she was close to childbirth. The lady left the bedside for a moment to try to calm down the dogs barking in an unusual way in the courtyard. At this point, her labor pains began and she was compelled to deliver in precarious conditions, helped by the only person on hand at that time, the steward, that is to say the family administrator. Everything went well and the woman had enough strength to hold her creature, Giovanna, in her arms, climb up the stairs, and go back to her husband's room. But he died a few minutes later. Leonilde said that during the labor she saw in front of her and along the corridors of the mansion a Capuchin friar of reassuring appearance, but she could not distinguish if it was an apparition or a hallucination.

The episode, supported with copious documentation during the procedure for the canonization of the friar and confirmed by the testimony of the noble woman, acquires a bewildering and mysterious significance some decades later, when Marquise Giovanna, already a spiritual daughter of Padre Pio, receives from the confessor of the friar, Padre Agostino of San Marco in Lamis, a sheet of paper from a notebook written by the saint in 1905. At that time, Padre Pio was not a priest yet and was taking a course of philosophy in the monastery of Sant'Elia a Pianisi, in the province of Campobasso. He was 17 and he had entered the Capuchin Order only two years earlier. On that paper, which contained the handwriting confirmed by experts to belong to the friar, is the following:

> Days ago a peculiar episode happened to me. While I was in the choir together with Padre Anastasio, it was about 11:00 pm

---

[5] A city in the far north-eastern section of Italy.

of the 18th day of last month [January], at once I found myself
very far away, in a high-class home, where the father was dying
while a baby girl was being born. Mary Most Holy then appeared
to me and told me: I entrust this creature to you. She is a precious stone, untreated: work on her, polish her, and make her
as shining as possible because I want her someday to adorn me.
Do not doubt, she will come to you, but first you will meet her
in St. Peter's.

The writing coincides exactly with the account of the occurrence
of the birth of Giovanna and of the death of Giovanni Battista in
Udine. Not only that: Lady Leonilde, as a widow, moved to Rome
where her parents lived and where little Giovanna grew up. In 1922
the girl, already an adolescent, started manifesting the first doubts
about her faith. She decided to solve them by consulting a priest.
So, on a muggy afternoon in the Roman summer, she went with a
friend to St. Peter's, but she found all the confessionals empty. She
sighted among the isles a little friar; she ran after him and was able
to talk to him. It was a long conversation, which, however, did not
eliminate her anguish or resolve her doubts. A year later, Giovanna
heard for the first time of Padre Pio and, following a mysterious
drive, she went in pilgrimage to San Giovanni Rotondo.

Marquise Giovanna recalled her meeting with the friar with
the stigmata this way:

> In the small monastery of San Giovanni Rotondo we found
> many people. There were also several important personalities.
> The corridor leading from the sacristy to the cloistered part of
> the monastery was packed. I was able to find room in the front.
> Passing by, Padre Pio stopped in front of me.
> He looked at me straight in the eyes and said smiling:
> "Giovanna, I know you. You were born on the same day your
> father died." The morning after I went to him for confession. As
> soon as I drew near, Padre Pio, after giving me the blessing, told
> me: "My daughter, finally you came. I have been waiting for you
> for many years." Then he added: "Last year on a summer after-
> noon, you went with a friend to the Basilica of St. Peter looking

for a priest who could enlighten you regarding your doubts on
the faith. You met a Capuchin and you spoke at length with him.
I was that Capuchin." After a brief pause, Padre Pio continued:
"When you were about to be born, the Blessed Mother took me
to the mansion. She made me witness the death of your father
and then she told me to take care of you. The Virgin entrusted
you to me and I have to take care of your soul."

From that moment on Giovanna became his spiritual daugh-
ter and for the rest of her life she went regularly to Padre Pio. She
was the only woman present, in the cell of the monastery of San
Giovanni Rotondo, at the moment of the death of Padre Pio, on
September 23, 1968. Giovanna Rizzani Boschi joined her friar in
Heaven ten years later.

The friar and the general

Padre Pio is an undisputed protagonist in the history of Italy.
It would be impossible to recount the events of the 20th century
without the existence of the friar of Pietrelcina. Padre Pio is a protagonist of our past also because this Capuchin became part of the
history taught by the books and in the classrooms on his own terms.
During the First World War, after the disastrous defeat at
Caporetto,[6] the commander-in-chief of the Italian army, General
Luigi Cadorna, succumbed to great despair. He knew that the
press and public opinion blamed him for the terrible defeat, and
he was crushed by the shame of that mark of infamy which fell
upon him and which, in reality, still rests on him today, despite
the fact that many historians maintain that the main responsibility for the ruinous retreat of Caporetto should be ascribed to the
young Pietro Badoglio.[7] Cadorna, then, was in the headquarters

---

[6] WWI started very inauspiciously for the Italian army, which was crushed by the
Austrian army in the early defeat at Caporetto.

[7] Badoglio was always shielded from blame mainly because of his Masonic con-
nections. He eventually became chief of staff. In fact, Italy's surrender in WWII
to the Allied forces was signed on behalf of Badoglio, who was then made Prime
Minister of Italy; he then consequently declared war on the former ally, Germany.

of the general staff in Treviso, guarded by three rows of sentinels. During the night, he drew the gun to his temple, with the intention of ending his life. At that point, the door opened and a bearded friar came in, never seen before, who evidently dissuaded him from the terrible act, and then left. The general, after the first moments of bewilderment, rushed to the sentry and asked harshly why he had violated his peremptory order not to let anyone come in. The soldier was astounded and swore again and again that no one had passed through there. A quick inquiry with all the other sentinels got the same result. Cadorna went back even more perplexed to his quarters, and put away his gun: the worst moment was now behind him. Only many years later, Cadorna saw the picture of Padre Pio on a magazine and recognized him as the friar of that night. Then, in civilian clothes, the elderly officer went to San Giovanni Rotondo. Despite the fact that he was among the crowd as a common pilgrim, when Padre Pio arrived in front of him, he stopped, and told him with a tone of complicity: "Hey general, tough time that night, wasn't it?"[8]

A special registered mail

There are plenty of stories of ordinary supernatural nature, at least in the life of this Capuchin, who lived his life fixed in place as much as he lived ubiquitously. He had a traumatized body and walked in a strange way, almost hopping on his wounded feet. But at the same time he would run across the world to be close to a soul in need. In the file of the inexplicable cases ascribed to Padre Pio, there are testimonies not only of bilocation, but also tens and hundreds of testimonies about healings, conversions, rescues from deadly perils, frightening accidents ending with no consequences. Of course, we can always have doubts about some circumstances, some rushed attributions, some emotional and sentimental exaggerations. This is legitimate and even reasonable, but, is it pos-

---

[8] These words were also spoken in the vernacular, as Padre Pio often did.

sible to dismiss everything as a huge manifestation of collective superstition?

For instance, the case of Carmela Catania, who was extremely ill and to whom her doctor himself had suggested the "therapy of desperation": to pray to Padre Pio. Carmela healed suddenly, amongst sweet aromas.

Let us consider another case, the one of Tony Colette in Houston, stricken by a very rare case of lipidosis which attacks the nervous and muscular systems. The surgeons had attempted several operations, but in the end gave up and sent the patient home to die. Tony prayed to Padre Pio, who appeared to him in a dream, and healed him.

Are these the deceptions of simple souls and frail minds? Is it the triumph of an immature and ignorant Catholicism? It was not really a naïve and illiterate Wanda Poltawska, a Polish psychiatrist who during the Second World War had been deported to Auschwitz, imprisoned for five years, and subjected to atrocious experiments. Despite all, she miraculously survived, started a family with Andrej Poltawsky, also a doctor, and had four daughters. In 1962, however, Wanda became ill: throat cancer. There was no hope for her, but the doctors decided to operate anyway.

On November 17 of the same year the Bishop of Krakow, at that time Monsignor Karol Wojtila, wrote to Padre Pio. The interesting thing is that the letter was written in the language of the Church: Latin. The future pope asked Padre Pio to pray "so that God, with the intervention of the Most Blessed Virgin, may show mercy to her and to her family." The letter was hand-carried by car to the friar by Honorable Angelo Battisti, an employee of the Vatican, who at that time was also the administrator of the Casa Sollievo della Sofferenza, and thus he had free access to the friar with the stigmata.

Padre Pio received Battisti while he was in prayer; he told him to open the envelope and read the message. After listening, he said:

"Angiolì,[9] I cannot say no to this requester." The honorable messenger remained speechless: how important could that Polish bishop be whom he had never heard of before? He would understand it years later when that man appeared at the window in St. Peter's Square clothed in the pope's vestment. One thing is absolutely certain: on November 21, before her surgery, Wanda Poltawska was suddenly healed. She could then continue to fight in defense of life and family, as she had done until then. She had fought against the pro-abortion law, which was passed in Poland in 1957. Wanda explained many years later that at the time of her healing she had never heard of Padre Pio. Then she knew nothing about this striking sentence of the friar with the stigmata regarding the subject of abortion:

> One day without abortions would be sufficient for God to grant peace on earth until the end of times.

A thorny sentence, spoken by a thorny man. How much easier would it have been to tolerate this Capuchin if he had had no bilocation, no miracles, no Latin Mass, no strict observance to the rules of the monastery, had he not displayed that humor showing the pleasant kindness of traditional Catholicism. But facts are obstinate, and these events actually occurred, in absolute reality.

---

[9] Familiar form for "Angelo."

CHAPTER 5

Behold Thy Mother

Padre Pio says Mass, does penance,
prays, hears Confessions, and is happy to be a child
in the arms of the Blessed Virgin Mary

"I am only a friar who prays," said Padre Pio about himself. Indeed, this could be a great epitaph, the perfect synthesis of the personality of the Saint of Pietrelcina. Maybe God willed to give him to us for this reason. Even today's believers, overwhelmed by the vortex of secularization and theological trends that have wiped out the importance of prayer, are compelled to look at the wounds on his hands, at his gift of bilocation, at the miracles, at the scents. And finally, to take notice of his life of unceasing prayer.

All this was fruit of the solid Marian root in which Padre Pio anchored his priestly life: "Only by linking Mary to your priesthood will you become effective in the field of grace, so as to have sons of God and saints germinate on earth." Who, if not a priest who teaches and practices such a confidence in Mary, could stay at the feet of the Cross and contemplate the greatness of the sentence "Behold thy mother" pronounced by the dying Jesus?

This moment of Calvary, so painful and so intimate, flourishes in the priestly life of Padre Pio, in his Mass, in his being, in the confessional, in his prayer, in his suffering, in his penance: a flower so beautiful that inspires and animates us.

The Mass is the true miracle

One day, a priest went to San Giovanni Rotondo to go to Confession to the friar with the stigmata and to introduce to him a sick person. Truthfully, his Confession did not seem to be anything extraordinary, and the sick person did not heal. Nevertheless, one thing shocked the priest: the Mass of the Padre. From that day on, the priest said, he would never again "get the Mass over with" as an automatic and routine deed. That priest had gone to the monastery of the famous Capuchin looking, perhaps, for something extraordinary. He found it, but not where he expected to find it. Not in the confessional, where not infrequently the friar demonstrated the knowledge of the sins of the penitent before he opened his mouth. He did not find it in the longed for healing capabilities of the persona, which had brought sudden healing to so many people. There was something extraordinary for sure, but it's impact was hidden in what he himself, as a priest, was doing every day: changing the bread and wine into the Body, Blood, Soul, and Divinity of Jesus Christ.

That was the daily miracle of Padre Pio, the one that everyone could see, just by going before dawn up to the little church of the monastery in San Giovanni Rotondo. The friar had said this many times: "The Most Holy Eucharist is the greatest of all miracles: it is the ultimate and greatest sign of the love of Jesus for us."

And again: "I can do three things at the same time: pray, give confession, and go around in the world." As a matter of fact, Padre Pio was essentially this: a friar who prayed, and who helped the souls by going, if necessary, to "meet" them in person through the mysterious instrument of bilocation. Obviously, at the summit of all prayers, was the Mass.

A drama, not a pop-fest

The Mass of Padre Pio is the heart of his spirituality. Whoever was able to attend one came out of this experience profoundly shaken. Illustrious witnesses have written about it, sometimes shocked. One of them, for example, was the sport reporter Orio Vergani, he who had followed, 25 times, the Tour of Italy and the

Tour de France, describing in memorable detail the portraits of the bike champions.

Or his colleague Igor Man, who, on February 1949, set out to San Giovanni Rotondo, and so described what he saw:

> At dawn, after spending the night smoking in a small hotel room, I attended Padre Pio's Mass. I was rarely going to church those days. [...] As in spring, when the wind caresses the wheat fields, bending the heads of the green ears, and the ears of wheat rippling as if whispering mysteries to one another, the heads of the faithful suddenly moved with a start, and a murmur traveled through the nave. Padre Pio was approaching the altar. He was walking slowly, with that difficult gait that made him drag his feet; his bent shoulders seemed to be the premonition of an unknown load. His hands holding the chalice and the paten were no longer covered by the woolen knitted gloves so that the stigmata, of a merciless red color, stood out on the white laces of the rochet. The sight of that blood is a revelation, almost. It leaves you breathless for an instant. Padre Pio slowly ascends the altar. He kneels painfully, as if bent under an enormous weight pushing slowly upon his head. He gets up with difficulty, pale. He signs himself with the sign of the Cross using those hands that look like wax, so beautiful and so shattered. An *ex voto*.[1] Now he entwines his fingers, closes his eyes, his eyelids tighten close together as if a blinding light beams on his face. He looks thinner and older; tired and distant. Terribly distant, stiffened in a grip of ineffable pain. [...] One feels that he is so immersed in the rite that he is unaware of the faithful.

The Mass of Padre Pio was extremely long; it could last even two hours. "The Padre" writes Rino Camilleri in his biography of the saint

> ... while celebrating, was extremely pale, with his eyes half-closed as if stunned by too much light. At the elevation, not a

---

[1] Common abbreviation for *ex voto suscepto* [from a vow made]. *Ex votos* are usually objects placed in a church or other sacred place in testimony of graces received or in fulfillment of vows made.

sound could be heard from the faithful, not even the shuffling of feet. And yet the church was always overfilled to the point of agony, despite the early hour, the mud, the snow. Everyone could see the Padre as if cut out of the rest of the world, afflicted by a consuming fire, mystically united to the Eternal Priest.

Besides, the Mass of Padre Pio did not lend itself so much to be described: it needed to be seen, to understand at least something about it. Padre Pio had a very distinctive deportment. It might be that he shook his head with abrupt movements, as if to fight off some invisible presence that was trying to prevent him from reciting the Consecration. "At the *Confiteor*" writes Camilleri with consistency,

> . . . his face had an expression of total annihilation, at the *Misereatur* he was almost in ecstasy, at the *Domine non sum dignus* the strokes on his chest echoed in the silence. Now the various parts of the Mass were clear to all the bystanders: that it was really the repetition of the sacrifice of Christ, not a boring and banal entertainment at the rhythmic beat of guitars and sometimes piteously enlivened by some improvisation of the priest.

There is indeed an enormous difference between the liturgy of the Capuchin with the stigmata and the Masses that have been forced upon us since the reform after the Vatican II Council. It has been a process of a progressive and inexorable trivialization, which has literally emptied the celebration of its contents, and has made of it a little show played on a theme, light years removed from the majestic and, at the same time, essential spectacle of the ancient rite.

Crisis of the Church, and crisis of the priesthood

It has often been said in our time that the Church is in crisis, but the courage has been lacking to strive to reach the core of this phenomenon: the unheard-of crisis of the priesthood and of the priests.

This is a crisis that did not materialize by pure chance, but that has been prepared and favored by decades of evil theology, a theology which has put the priest at the same level as any of the other baptized, which has insisted pathologically on the existence of a universal priesthood of the faithful, which has mortified and made insignificant the ministerial priesthood.

Furthermore, such theology has demotivated young people from becoming priests, if, after all, to be a lay person or to be a priest is the same thing. Such theology has been the Trojan horse of Protestant thinking and praxis, which from Luther on, indeed, has been existing without the true role of priests. A large section of Catholicism following Vatican Council II, has literally begun to pursue that model, constructing a Church without priests. Unfortunately, this project, in reality, is the continuation of the empty classrooms in the diocesan seminaries.

The Catholic Church is in crisis because the priesthood is in crisis. On April 1, 1987, John Paul II pronounced words indicating his awareness of this state of things:

> A priest is worth as much as his Eucharistic life is worth, first of all his Mass. Mass without love, fruitless priest. If his Mass is passionate, the priest conquers souls. If the Eucharistic devotion is neglected and unloved, the priest is in peril, languishing and declining.

Benedict XVI had the great merit and the courage, to give to this reality a formal recognition, making of it the heart of his pontificate. He was the one who announced an extraordinary year of the priesthood, which, not by chance, some dioceses have tried to neutralize by explaining to the faithful that it was about reflecting "upon the meaning of one's baptism." This is what was said over and over, for example, in the diocese of Milan.

It was the same Benedict XVI who concluded the year of the priesthood by delivering a homily in St. Peter's Square on June 11, 2010, in which he pronounced words heavy like stones:

We must let the Curé of Ars guide us, to understand again the greatness and the beauty of the priestly ministry.

The choice of the Curé of Ars as a model for the priest of the third millennium is shocking, since John Marie Vianney essentially did only the following: celebrated Mass, prayed, heard Confessions, preached, and did penance. Nothing more, nothing less. Just as Padre Pio of Pietrelcina, who used to say: "The Lord elects the priest for the altar and the confessional."

In that speech of June 2010, Benedict XVI further explains:

> The priest is not simply the one in charge of an office, like those needed in every society to accomplish certain tasks. Instead, he does something which no other human being can do on his own: he pronounces in the name of Christ the word of the absolution from our sins, thus changing, with power proceeding from God, the status of our life. He pronounces on the offering of the bread and the wine the words of thanksgiving of Christ, which are words of transubstantiation—words which make present in person the Resurrected One, His body and His blood, and so that they change the elements of the world: words that open the world to God and join it to Him.

The priest, says the pope, is profoundly different from all the other faithful. His duty is also different from every other human assignment or responsibility:

> The priesthood is, therefore, not simply an "office," but a sacrament: God uses a poor man in order to be, through him, present to men and to act in their favor. This is the audacity of God, who entrusts Himself to human beings; Who, even knowing our weaknesses, trusts some men capable of acting and being present in His stead, this audacity of God is the truly great thing hidden under the word "priesthood."

The priest, continues the pope, is one who carries on his shoulders the destiny of the souls that the Eternal Father committed to his care:

God wills that we, as priests, in a little point in history, share His concern for men. As priests, we would like to be people who, in communion with His solicitude for men, care for them, make them experience tangibly this attentiveness of God.

A priest does not really love his flock if he lets heresy, the misrepresentation, and the decline of the faith flourish, as if we could autonomously invent the faith.

The hidden tabernacle

If the Mass is a service which the priest, as a functionary, must provide to the clientele, then it is sufficient to supply the package at the established time, arriving at the right place on time to start.

Padre Pio, instead, began preparing for Mass at 2:30 am. Then, at 4 am, he would go down to the church, already overflowing with the faithful waiting for him. With a few eloquent gestures he hushed everyone, extinguishing any inappropriate chatter.

In church, one must behave appropriately; because the church is not the gathering place of a Protestant community, or the neutral theatre that hosts the celebration of the rite. The church is the abode of the Tabernacle, and, therefore, it is the house of Our Lord. In Padre Pio's time this concept was clear; proof of it was the unequivocal location of the Tabernacle, situated exactly in the focal point of every Catholic church, so that, upon entering no faithful could avoid seeing it, and make the due genuflection.

The same is not the case in many modern churches, where the Tabernacle has been literally hidden in some side chapel, or placed in a position hiding it from the direct sight of the faithful.

The utmost paradox, one of the most blatant examples of the new architecture, is certainly the gigantic church recently built at San Giovanni Rotondo. It would be difficult to imagine a building further removed from Tridentine sensitivity and from absolute fidelity to tradition, which characterized the saint with the stigmata.

The architectural structure designed by Renzo Piano is, from the view point of Catholic standards, embarrassing. The embarrassment arises if you add to it the disquieting symbols used in the decoration of the building, which more than one expert has linked to freemasonry. Those responsible for such choices decline with disdain every criticism voiced to the temple and every reference to the lodges. One question remains unanswered: Would this new "church" have pleased Padre Pio of Pietrelcina? Would the saint ever have approved the building of a sacred place having that shape and those decorations?

The house of Our Lord

All of the saint's writings show that for that simple and sturdy friar, who was firm and unwavering, the church was a place that should conform to some indispensable and essential prerequisites, starting from the altar, on which was placed the Tabernacle, and toward which the priest would normally celebrate Mass.

In 1913, he himself transcribed, in a letter written to his spiritual director, the words spoken by Jesus in one of his visions: "My house has become for many a house of entertainment."

Padre Pio of Pietrelcina demanded that the faithful show the respect due in church, and he took care to give very precise directions in this regard. On July 25, 1915, the saint writes to his spiritual daughter Anita Rodote:

> In the house of God, in the church, which the Divine Master likes to call "house of prayer," I exhort you in the Lord to practice the following:
>
> Enter the church in silence and with great respect, considering and holding yourself as unworthy to come before the majesty of the Lord. Among the other devout considerations, think that our soul is the temple of God, and that as such we have to preserve it pure and clean in front of God and His angels.
>
> Take then the holy water and make well and slowly the sign of our redemption: the sign of the Cross.

As soon as you see God in the Blessed Sacrament (there is an altar where the Eucharist is preserved: it is marked by a burning lamp), devoutly genuflect, bending your knee to the ground; first greet Him, your Lord—living and real in the tabernacle—then the Blessed Mother and the saints.

After you find your place, kneel down and render to Jesus in the Blessed Sacrament the offer of your prayer and your adoration. Disclose to Him all the needs of yourself and others, talk to Him with filial abandonment, freely unburden your heart and give Him complete sovereignty to operate in you as He pleases.

When attending Holy Mass and the sacred liturgies, use much propriety in standing up, in kneeling, in sitting down, and make any religious action with the greatest devotion. Be modest in your gazes; do not turn your head here and there to see who comes in and who goes out; do not laugh, in reverence to the holy place and also in regard to your neighbors; refrain from exchanging any word with anyone, unless demanded by charity or by a true necessity.

If you pray with others, pronounce distinctly the words of the prayer, make the pauses properly, do not use a high tone of voice, never rush, and follow the pace of the priest who leads and of the others.

In summary, behave in such a way that all the bystanders may be edified and may be led by you to glorify and love the heavenly Father.

As you go out of the church keep an absorbed and calm behavior: first take leave from Jesus in the Blessed Sacrament, ask Him forgiveness for the faults committed in His divine presence, and never depart from Him before asking and obtaining from Him the fatherly blessing.

After exiting the church, behave as any follower of the Nazarene should.

The advice of Padre Pio to today's man

A little bit of familiarity with the Sunday Masses of our day and age makes us aware of the abyss now separating the good advice of Padre Pio from today's customary practices.

Perhaps priests would do well to pick up again this list of wise observations, and fill up their homilies with this blessed material. Maybe they should start over by re-educating from scratch their uninhibited customary faithful. Perhaps they should work to give back to the church the dignity owed to the house of Our Lord, too often turned into a "den of thieves," where people talk and make a racket as if it were the village square. Perhaps the time has come to substitute the bizarre and often incomprehensible biblical exegesis, which never converted anyone and which changes the homilies into soporific conferences for the experts, with a renewed life of piety, consisting of very tangible deeds and concrete behavior.

A starting point could be the parishioners' clothing, by reminding the Christians that when they go to church they go to meet the King of kings, and that the proper attire for the church must be kept separate from the one for free time or for the beach. We could go on talking about punctuality, as even when we are invited at the house of someone much less important than Christ, we take care to get there on time.

We could go on with many other simple guidelines: let us avoid going to Communion if we are in mortal sin, because, as the apostle Paul says: "Whosoever shall eat this bread, or drink the chalice of the Lord unworthily [...] eats and drinks judgment to himself" (I Cor. 11:27-29).

Let us listen in silence to the words of the Mass that only the priest must pronounce; avoid repeating them out loud, or even in a low voice. Let us learn to stay kneeling during the entire time of Consecration and after receiving the Eucharist. St. John Bosco recommended:

> After Holy Communion, remain at least one quarter of an hour for the Thanksgiving. It would be a grave irreverence if, a few minutes after receiving the Body-Blood-Soul-Divinity of Jesus, one left the church or, remaining in his place, started laughing, chitchatting, or looking around here and there in the church.

From his point of view, Padre Pio did not go immediately into the confessional after the Mass, but he devoted himself for about one hour to the Thanksgiving, first in the Sacristy, where he used to stop with his head leaning on a kneeling-stool, and then into the chapel inside the monastery.

Fifty rosaries a day

"In the books we search for God. In prayer we find Him." Padre Pio had clear ideas in this regard. It is not by chance that, besides the Mass, fulcrum and center of every prayer, the saint had a Marian devotion which literally devoured him. Padre Stefano M. Manelli is a Franciscan, founder of the congregation of the Franciscan Friars of the Immaculata. He spent time with Padre Pio since his infancy, and he recalls that the Saint of Pietrelcina had a very special veneration for the Blessed Mother. Padre Manelli tells us that: "Padre Pio had the habit of reciting the rosary everywhere: in his cell, in the hallways, in the sacristy, going up and down the stairs, night and day."

Someone asked Padre Pio how many rosaries he recited in one night and one day. "Sometimes 40 and other times 50," he answered with extreme simplicity. Facing the surprise of his interlocutor, he added: "How can you do without reciting them?"

According to Padre Pio, the rosary is a very powerful weapon, extremely hated by the enemy: "Satan aims at destroying this prayer, but he will never succeed." Other times he would say: "Let us empty Purgatory" while taking hold of the rosary beads. It was his favorite prayer because it is the favorite prayer of Our Lady, to whom he had associated his priesthood. He told his spiritual director in a letter: "I would like to have a voice so loud to be able to invite all the sinners in the world to love Our Lady. But, as this is not in my power, I prayed my little angel to accomplish this task for me." And in another letter he said: "I would like to be able to fly to invite all human beings to love Mary."

Therefore, the Padre had a great and affectionate love for the rosary. He petitioned to recite it in substitution of the Divine Office as a young friar, when he was sick and unable to read. This was granted to him also when he was near the end of his life and his eyes were failing. He may have blessed those infirmities that allowed him to fill his empty time between the confessional and the altar reciting this marvelous recursive rhyme which is nothing but the story of Jesus as told by Mary.

Besides showing the beauty and efficacy of it, he also taught how to recite it:

> You must put your attention on the *Ave,* on the greeting you address to the Virgin in the mystery you are contemplating. In all the mysteries She was present, in all of them She participated with love and sorrow.

One day, a confrere told him: "Nowadays they say that the rosary is outdated…in many churches they no longer recite it." And he in reply:

> Satan always aims at destroying this prayer, but he will never succeed: it is the prayer of She who triumphs over all and over everyone. She is the one who taught it to us, like Jesus taught us the *Pater Noster.*

Shortly before his death, some confreres asked him to say something to console them. And he, with his gaze already toward Heaven: "Love the Blessed Mother and make others love her. Recite the rosary always."

The Blessed Mother was his sure guide. To Her he entrusted himself in order to be a priest worthy to be considered an *Alter Christus*:

> Only by associating Mary to your priesthood will you become effective in the field of the grace, to grow sons of God and saints of the earth.

Chronology

1887

May 25: Born in Pietrelcina (in the province of Benevento, Italy), the son of Orazio Forgione, commonly called Grazio, and Maria Giuseppa Di Nunzio. On the following day he was baptized and given the name of Francesco.

1899

Sometime during this year he received First Communion. *September 27*: He received Confirmation.

1903

January 1 to 5: He received three visions revealing his future.

January 6: He entered the novitiate of the Capuchin Friars in Morcone (in the Province of Benevento, Italy).

January 22: he took the habit.

1904

January 22: He was admitted to simple religious profession. Three days later he left for Sant'Elia a Pianisi (in the Province of Campobasso) to attend the Gymnasium [Junior High].

1905

In the monastery of Santa Maria del Monte in Campobasso he received numerous apparitions of the Virgin Mary.

August 15: The Blessed Mother showed him that his mission would be that of an *Alter Christus*.

1907

January 27: He pronounced his solemn vows in the monastery of Sant'Elia a Pianisi.

By the end of October he took up studies in Theology in Serracapriola (in the province of Foggia). His teacher was Padre Agostino of San Marco in Lamis.

1908

December 19: In the cathedral of Benevento he received the tonsure and the minor orders. Two days later he received the sub-diaconate.

1909

During the first part of this year he was compelled to return to Pietrelcina because of ill-health.

July 18: He was ordained deacon in the friary church of Morcone.

1910

July 30: He passed the exams for the priestly ordination.

August 10: He received priestly ordination in the canons' chapel of Benevento.

August 14: He celebrated his first Mass in Pietrelcina. In the month of September he received the invisible stigmata.

1911

By the end of October his health conditions became worse and he was obliged, one more time, to return to Pietrelcina, where he remained, except for a few short periods of time, from the month of December until February 1916.

1915

November 6: He reported to the military recruiting office in Benevento to fulfill his duty as a citizen, but he was sent home on convalescent leave.

1916

July 28: He arrived for the first time in San Giovanni Rotondo, supposedly to find out if the climate there would be more suitable for his health. Until 1918 he could not find a long-term residence: he had to present himself several times at the military barracks in Naples, as the military authorities did not consider his health conditions sufficiently severe.

1918

March 16: He was discharged from the army as a result of double broncheo-alvolitis.

March 18: He returned to the monastery in San Giovanni Rotondo.

August 5 to 7: From a mysterious figure he received the transverberation, a wound in his heart continuously bleeding.

September 20: While praying in the choir, he received the stigmata in his hands, feet, and side.

December 20: The phenomenon of the transverberation occurred again.

1919

May 15 to 17: He underwent a medical examination by Dr. Luigi Romanelli, head physician of the hospital in Barletta, to assess the nature of the wounds he had received. In July, sent by the Vatican, he was examined by Prof. Amico Bignami, of the University of Rome. In October, he was examined by Dr. Giorgio Festa, sent by the Capuchin Superior General.

1920

April 18: Padre Agostino Gemelli arrived in San Giovanni Rotondo demanding to see the wounds of Padre Pio even though he had received no written order to do so. Padre Pio refused to show them to him. Nonetheless, the founder of the Catholic University of the Sacred Heart, who was highly esteemed in the scientific field, sent the Vatican a heavily negative report regarding the phenomenon of the stigmata and the person of the Padre.

1921

The report of Padre Gemelli unleashed a storm upon Padre Pio. Rumors circulated about Padre Pio being transferred to Spain; the inhabitants of San Giovanni Rotondo rose up in rebellion.

October 25: Cardinal Augusto Silj and Monsignor Giuseppe De Angeli arrived in San Giovanni Rotondo to appease the population.

1922

June 2: The first persecution of Padre Pio officially began. The Holy Office sanctioned a series of restrictions upon the friar with the stigmata, and forced him to change his spiritual director.

1923

May 31: The Holy Office decreed that the facts regarding Padre Pio did not consist of a supernatural nature.

June 17: Padre Pio was obliged to celebrate Mass in the inner chapel of the monastery, with no faithful allowed to attend. He also was forbidden to reply to the letters he received.

1926

January 5: The Canon Giovanni Miscio was arrested. He had been a close coadjutor of the Archbishop of Manfredonia, Monsignor Pasquale Gagliardi, unrelenting enemy of Padre Pio. Subsequently, the shady conspiracies were unveiled, which reached from the Archbishop's office all the way to the monastery of San Giovanni Rotondo.

1927

March 26: Monsignor Felice Bevilacqua was sent to San Giovanni Rotondo for an apostolic visit. The year after there was to be another one by Monsignor Giuseppe Bruno.

1929

January 3: Padre Pio's mother died in San Giovanni Rotondo. In the fall the Archbishop of Manfredonia was suspended from his appointment.

1931

June 9: Padre Pio was notified of his suspension from all priestly ministries, except for the celebration of the Holy Mass, which had to take place strictly in private and in the presence of the server alone.

1933

March 14: Padre Pio received the visit of Monsignor Luca Pasetto and Monsignor Felice Bevilacqua. The situation improved.

July 16: Padre Pio returned to celebrate the Mass publicly.

1934

March 25: Padre Pio resumed the hearing of men's confessions.

May 12: He resumed the hearing of women's confessions.

1946

October 7: Padre Pio's father died in San Giovanni Rotondo.

1947

May 19: In San Giovanni Rotondo, the construction of the hospital *Casa Sollievo Della Sofferenza* [Home for the Relief of Suffering] began, which would be inaugurated on May 5, 1956.

1957

April 4: Pope Pius XII designated Padre Pio as the director for life of the third order Franciscan fraternity "Santa Maria delle Grazie" and appointed him to guide the hospital "Casa Sollievo della Sofferenza."

1959

April 25: Padre Pio fell grievously ill, with no hope for recovery. He will miraculously heal during August 5 and 6, when the pilgrim statue of Our Lady of Fatima came to San Giovanni Rotondo; to her the friar attributed his miraculous cure.

1960

Monsignor Carlo Maccari arrived in San Giovanni Rotondo for a new apostolic visit. The second persecution began. The action came from within the Capuchin order itself. Under the pretext of disciplining Padre Pio, they sought to withdraw from him the considerable monetary offers coming in for the *Casa Sollievo della Sofferenza*. The action was initiated because many authorities in the Capuchin order were found to be financially involved in the Giuffré affair [a scandal involving the Vatican Bank].

1964

January 23: The new Father Guardian of the monastery of San Giovanni Rotondo, Padre Carmelo of San Giovanni in Galdo, delivered the order from Pope Paul VI to return Padre Pio to full freedom in his ministry.

May 11: Padre Pio designated the Holy See as the sole heir of all his possessions.

1965

March 9: Cardinal Antonio Bacci arrived in San Giovanni Rotondo to deliver to Padre Pio the indult to continue to celebrate the Mass according to the old rite. The friar had asked to be allowed to celebrate the Mass of all times after seeing the first liturgical innovations, which culminated in the reform of 1969.

1968

September 20: From a picture taken during the celebration of the Mass, it seemed that the stigmata on the right hand of Padre Pio had disappeared.

September 22: Padre Pio celebrated his last Mass.

September 23: Padre Pio died at 2:31 am. The stigmata on his body had completely disappeared.

1999

May 2: Padre Pio was proclaimed Blessed.

2002

June 16: Padre Pio was proclaimed Saint.

Bibliography

Pio da Pietrelcina, *Epistolario*, eds. Melchiorre da Pobladura and Alessandro da Ripabottoni. (Padre Pio da Pietrelcina Editions, San Giovanni Rotondo, four volumes, 1973-1974).

—————, *Lavori scolastici*, ed. Fr. Gerardo Di Flumeri. (Padre Pio da Pietrelcina Editions, San Giovanni Rotondo, 1993).

—————, *Solo, nel mistero di Dio: Sinossi ascetico-mistico da tutti gli scritti*, ed. Silvano Pannunzio. (Cantagalli Editions, Siena, 1992).

Ss. Vv. *Fonti francescane*. Franciscan Editions.

Allegri, R. *Padre Pio: Un santo tra noi*. Mondadori.

Amorth, G. *Padre Pio: Breve storia di un santo*. Bologna, Italy: Dehoniane Editions.

Beretta, R. *Il lungo autunno*. Rizzoli.

Breve esame critico del Novus Ordo Missae. Una Voce.

Cammilleri, R. *Vita di Padre Pio*. Piemme.

Castelli, F. *Padre Pio sotto inchiesta: L'autobiografia segreta*. Ares.

Castello, N. and S. M. Manelli. *La "Dolce Signora" di Padre Pio: Il mistero di Maria nella vita del beato di Pietrelcina*. San Paolo.

Castello, N., S. M. Manelli, and A. Negrisolo. *Padre Pio nella sua interiorità*. San Paolo.

Castello, N. and A. Negrisolo. *Il beato Padre Pio: Miracolo eucaristico*. San Paolo.

Chiocci, F. and L. Cirri. *Padre Pio: Storia di una vittima*. I Libri del no.

Chiron, Y. *Padre Pio: Una strada di Misericordia*. Paoline Editions.

D'Apolito, A. *Padre Pio da Pietrelcina: Ricordi, esperienze, testimonianze*. Padre Pio da Pietrelcina Editions.

Da Cervinar,a T. *La Messa di Padre Pio*. Convent of the Capuchins of San Giovanni Rotondo.

Da Riese Pio X. F. *Padre Pio da Pietrelcina: Crocifisso senza croce*. Padre Pio da Pietrelcina Editions.

Da Ripabottoni, A. *Padre Pio da Pietrelcina: Profilo biografico*. Padre Pio da Pietrelcina Editions.

—————. *Padre Pio da Pietrelcina: Il "cireneo di tutti."* Padre Pio da Pietrelcina Editions.

Di Flumeri, G., editor. *Le stigmata di Padre Pio da Pietrelcina: testimonianze, relazioni*. Padre Pio da Pietrelcina Editions.

——————. *La transverberazione di Padre Pio da Pietrelcina*. Padre Pio da Pietrelcina Editions.

Guéranger, Dom Prosper. "De vita contemplativa." *La Santa Messa*.

——————. *L'eresia antiliturgica e la riforma protestante*. Amicizia Cristiana.

Iasenzaniro, M. *Padre Pio: Profilo di un santo*. Padre Pio da Pietrelcina Editions.

Ireneo di Lione. *Contro le eresie*. In: *L'Anticristo: Il nemico dei tempi finali*. Vol. 1. Fondazione Valla-Mondadori.

Lauriola, A. C. *L'amore più grande: Padre Pio da Petrelcina*. Libreria Editrice Vaticana.

Manelli, M. C. P. "San Francesco, zelatore della liturgia romana." *Annales Franciscani* (Casa Mariana Editrice, 2009).

Manelli, S. M. "Il motu proprio Summorum Pontificum per la crescita della vita religiosa." In: *Atti del Convegno "Il Motu proprio Summorum Pontificum, un grande dono per la Chiesa."* (2009).

——————. *San Pio da Pietrelcina*. Casa Mariana Editrice.

Pasquale, G. *Padre Pio: Modello di vit sacerdotale*. San Paolo.

——————. *Padre Pio: Sperare oltre il soffrire*. Jaca Book.

Pasquale, G., editor. *Padre Pio: Maestro e guida dell'anima*. San Paolo.

Peroni, L. *Padre Pio da Pietrelcina*. Borla.

——————. *Padre Pio: Il san Francesco dei nostri tempi*. Borla.

——————. *I miei incontri con Padre Pio*. Borla.

Preziuso, G. *Padre Pio: Apostolo del confessionale*. San Paolo.

Pronzato, A. *Padre Pio: Mistero gaudioso*. Gribaudi.

——————. *Padre Pio: Mistero doloroso*. Gribaudi.

——————. *Padre Pio: Mistero glorioso*. Gribaudi.

Socci, A. *Il segreto di Padre Pio*. Rizzoli.

Tangari, K. *Il messaggio di Padre Pio*. Amis de saint Francois de Sales edition.

Tosatti, M. *Quando la Chiesa perseguitava Padre Pio*. Piemme.

Winowska, M. *Il vero volto di Padre Pio*. Edizioni Paoline.